The Independent Mind

Extemporaneous talks given by Osho in Mumbai, India

The Independent Mind

LEARNING TO LIVE A LIFE OF FREEDOM

Originally published in Hindi as *Chit Chakmak Lage Nahin*. The material in this
book is a series of talks by Osho given to a live audience. The complete OSHO text
archive can be found via the online OSHO Library at www.osho.com/Library

OSHO MEDIA INTERNATIONAL
New York • Zurich • Mumbai
an imprint of
OSHO INTERNATIONAL
www.osho.com/oshointernational

Library of Congress Catalog-In-Publication Data is available

Printed in India by Manipal Technologies Limited, Karnataka

ISBN: 978-1-938755-79-8
This title is also available in eBook format ISBN: 978-0-88050-083-8

contents

Your thoughts are not yours – you have gathered them together. Sometimes in a dark room, a beam of light comes from the roof and you can see millions of dust particles floating in that beam. When I look into you I see the same phenomenon: millions of dust particles. You call them thoughts. They are moving in you and out of you. From one head they enter another and on they go. They have their own life.

A thought is a thing; it has its own existence. When a person dies, all his mad thoughts are released immediately and they start finding shelter somewhere or other. They immediately enter those who are nearby. They are like germs, they have their own life. Even when you are alive you go on dispersing your thoughts all around you. When you talk, of course you throw your thoughts into others. But when you are silent, you also throw thoughts around. They are not yours; that is the first thing.

A man of positive reasoning will discard all thoughts that are not his own. They are not authentic, he hasn't found them through his own experience. He has accumulated them from others, they are borrowed. They are dirty, and have been in many hands and in many heads. A man of thinking does not borrow, he likes to have fresh thoughts of his own. If you are positive, and look at beauty, truth, goodness, flowers; if you become capable of seeing even in the darkest night that the morning is approaching – you will become capable of thinking.

You can then create your own thoughts. A thought that is created by you is really full of potential; it has a power of its own.

Osho
Yoga: The Science of the Soul, Vol 2

CHAPTER 1

discovering life

My beloved ones.

In the coming three days I will talk to you about the search for life. Before I begin talking about this search – from tomorrow morning onward – I must first say that life is not what we understand it to be. Until this is clear to us, and we recognize in our hearts that what we think of as life is not life at all, the search for the true life cannot begin.

If someone thinks darkness is light, he will not go in search of light. If someone thinks death is life, he will be deprived of life. If what we think and understand is wrong, the end result of our whole life is bound to be wrong. Our search will depend on our understanding. So the first thing I want to say is that very few people attain life. Everyone attains birth and most people mistakenly consider birth to be life. What we know as life is just an opportunity to discover life, to find life or to miss it. Through that opportunity we can find life, but we can also miss it.

What we know as life is only an opportunity, is just a possibility. It is a seed out of which something may or may not blossom. It is also possible that the seed may lie dormant, may not sprout. Flowers may not blossom out of it, it may not bear fruit; both possibilities are there.

Up to now, the seed of most people's life remains infertile. It is only in a very few people's lives that the seed sprouts, that flowers blossom, that fragrance comes. These are the few people we worship and remember. But we never remember one thing: we also have been given the same seed, we could also attain exactly the same fragrance.

Unless, when seeing people like Mahavira, Buddha, Krishna, and Christ, someone finds it humiliating that he too has the same seed within him and can attain the same life as theirs, all his worshipping and prayers are futile. They are a mere pretense, hypocrisy.

Just to avoid this suffering, just to avoid this pain, we have turned Krishna, Buddha, and Mahavira into "the blessed one" – into God. If they were ordinary human beings like us, we would be ashamed of being human beings. If they were just like us, there would be no place, no possibility, for us to escape. Just to avoid this humiliation, this pain and suffering, we have started calling them God, the son of God, *tirthankaras*, and who knows what. By calling them God, the son of God, or *tirthankara* we have imposed foolish things on them. All these people were just like us, were ordinary human beings. But most human-seeds are unable to blossom. Very few life-seeds blossom so perfectly that a divine light starts manifesting through them.

If religion has any purpose at all, it is this: all seeds should become what they are supposed to be, what is hidden within should become manifest. Unless we realize that what we are doing and the direction in which we are moving are completely wrong, no revolution, no transformation, no about-turn will be possible. This is the first thing I want to tell you today.

What we know as life is nothing more than a slow and gradual death, day by day. Such a lengthy death cannot be called life. If a man dies after seventy years, the process of death continues for seventy years. Someone may die after one hundred years, someone else after fifty years – we simply go on, quietly considering this lengthy process of death to be life. Today your life span is one day less than it was yesterday and tomorrow it will be less by one more day. What you think is an increase in age is actually a decreasing of age. The days you celebrate as birthdays are nothing but milestones indicating that death is coming closer. And after running in all directions, we find that in the end we have reached death.

We run in every possible direction, we take a thousand and one measures and make a thousand and one arrangements: we do anything and everything, but all our running around is nothing more than an attempt to avoid death. Someone may be accumulating wealth, someone may be accumulating fame, someone may be accumulating status, and someone may be trying to become more powerful; all these efforts are just to avoid that one thing. So when death comes, we have a defense, a security arrangement to protect ourselves against it. But all these arrangements fail. Death simply comes.

I am reminded of a short story…

An emperor from Damascus had a dream one night in which he saw himself standing next to his horse under a tree. A dark shadow came from behind and put its hand on his shoulder. When he turned and looked around, he became frightened.

The shadow said, "I am Death, and tomorrow I will be coming to take you, so be ready and make sure that you reach the chosen place."

He woke up, the dream disappeared, but he was afraid. When morning came, he called all the greatest and most famous astrologers of his kingdom. He called renowned scholars who could interpret dreams and asked them, "What does this dream mean? What does it indicate? Last night in my dream I saw a dark shadow that put its hand on my shoulder saying, 'I am Death and tomorrow I will come to take you, so be ready and make sure that you meet me at the chosen place.'"

There was not much time. He only had that day because Death would be arriving in the evening, at sunset. The astrologers said, "There is not much time to think. Just take the fastest horse you have and ride away from here as far as you can. The further away you can go the better."

There didn't seem to be any other option. What else could one think of? This was the only solution: he should go away as far as possible from that palace, from that state. What other way could there be to save himself? If someone had asked you, what could you have suggested? Or if someone had asked me, what else could I have said? Those astrologers advised rightly. Man's mind cannot think further than this, it cannot find a better solution. It was a clear-cut thing: he should ride away from the palace to save himself from Death.

The emperor obviously had no shortage of fast horses. He had the fastest and best. He called for one of the fastest horses, mounted it, and it started running. The horse ran at a fast speed and seeing this rapid speed, slowly, slowly the emperor became very relaxed in his mind. Naturally, he gained confidence: he would go as far as possible, now he would be saved.

Slowly, slowly the capital city was left far behind, his state was left far behind, towns and villages were left far behind. The horse continued running at the same fast pace. The emperor did not take a rest; he neither ate any food nor drank any water. Who would stop? Who would eat food or drink water when he was being chased by Death? And he did not give the horse a break either; he did not even arrange any water for it. It was essential for him to ride as far away as possible that day.

Afternoon came. The king had ridden far from his palace, he

was utterly happy. Up until the afternoon he had been sad, but by late afternoon he started humming songs. He had the feeling that now he had come far enough. By the time evening came he was hundreds of miles away.

Just as the sun was setting, he went into a nearby mango grove, tied up his horse and stood under a tree. He was utterly relaxed. He was about to express his thankfulness to God that he had come far enough, when the same hand that he had seen the night before in his dream touched his shoulder. He became frightened. He turned around carefully – and saw the same dark shadow standing there.

The dark shadow said to him, "I was very worried whether you'd be able to reach this far or not, as this is the place where you are destined to die. I was wondering how it would be possible for you to travel such a long distance. But your horse was so fast and you rode very well. You have come at the right time."

No matter how far we may run, it is going to happen. It makes no difference whether you have had the dream or not. This is bound to happen: one day you will meet death at the place where it is supposed to be met.

The directions we are running in may be different, our routes may be different and the speed of our horses may vary – this is possible. But ultimately it won't make much difference. Someday or other, under some tree, a hand will be placed on your shoulder. Then you will find yourself meeting the one you were running away from. That day you will feel frightened. In fact, you were only running toward that which you were trying to run away from. There is no way to escape death.

No matter where we may run, we only run toward death. The very running takes us to death. Whoever runs, will reach death. It is possible that a poor man may run very slowly. He does not have a horse, so he will have to run without a horse. A rich man may run with a bigger horse and the emperors may run with a fast horse. But eventually the people without horses will reach the same place – death – as the people with horses have reached. Then what is the solution? What is the path? What can be done?

The first thing I would like to tell you is that whatever you are doing will simply take you to death. This is nothing to be surprised about. Even in the past, whatever people have been doing has taken them to death. Very few people have escaped death. What they have done to transcend death you are not doing at all. Whatever preparations you are making, they are simply preparations for death. You may find this pleasant or unpleasant, but the truth is: all our preparations are nothing but preparation for death. In these three days, I would like to tell you what the signs of preparing for death are, and how preparations for life can be made.

It is possible that deep down you have the desire to know and discover life. In reality, there is not a single person who does not have the desire to find life. And yet there is some kind of madness, some deep madness which has afflicted the whole of humanity. As soon as a newborn child comes into the world, he is initiated into the same madness. Perhaps it is natural. If the child does not get initiated into it, he will appear mad to us. The day Mahavira left home, people thought him mad. The day Buddha ran away from home, he too was considered mad, and Christ was also thought to be madman. The whole of mankind is insane, so whenever a sane man is born, he is considered mad.

Perhaps you will understand my point better if I tell you a short story...

It happened that one day early in the morning an old woman came and threw something into the village well and announced that whoever drank water from that well would become mad. There were only two wells in the village. One was in the village itself and the other was in the king's palace. By evening, the whole village went mad as they had no choice but to drink water from their well. Only three people – the king, the queen, and the prime minister – did not drink the water from the village well, so they were saved from going mad.

A rumor spread around the village: it appears that the king has gone mad. And this is quite natural – when the whole village has gone mad, someone who is not mad will definitely appear mad to everyone else. This is simple arithmetic. So everyone in the village became very worried and disturbed. Among them, the ones who were great thinkers… Usually mad people are great thinkers. That is why there is much less of a gap between a mad person and a thinker: the thinkers often go mad and the mad often start thinking.

So among those mad people there were a few thinkers and a few politicians. They all assembled to decide what they should do. They thought that unless they removed the king, everything would be in a mess. "If the king is mad, who will run the kingdom?"

In the evening, they gathered outside the palace and shouted slogans saying that as the king had gone mad, the prime minister had gone mad, and the queen also, they now had no choice but to remove the king.

The king, his queen, and the prime minister stood on the roof of the palace contemplating what they should do. All their servants and the soldiers had also gone mad; everyone had gone mad, so what would happen now?

The king said to the prime minister, "Think quickly what we should do."

He said, "There is no way out except to immediately drink water from the village well."

All three of them told the people, "Wait, we will go and find something to treat our madness."

They went to the village well and drank the water. That night a great celebration took place in the village. People were dancing and singing: the king had come back to his senses.

Humanity is afflicted by a deep and fundamental insanity, and we initiate our new generation of children into that madness. All the children who refuse to be initiated will appear rebellious. The children who refuse to be initiated into that madness will appear mad to us, so to ensure that they also go mad, we force them onto the same path.

It is utterly dangerous to be sane in this world; a sane person has to pay a heavy price for his sanity. Someone has to face a bullet, someone else has to drink poison, another one has to be crucified. Sane people are not tolerated in a world full of mad people. In this world, the madder a person is, the more appealing he appears to be because he seems to be one of our own. He seems to be walking the same path we are walking on.

So I am going to talk to you about how to get rid of the state of deep madness that has its grip on humanity. If you don't try to find a way out, death will be the outcome. No matter what you do, in the end death will catch hold of you – not necessarily in the distant future. It can catch hold of you tomorrow, it can catch hold of you today. It can even catch hold of you right now.

So tonight think and contemplate on this: if whatever you are doing only takes you to death, then what is the significance in doing it? If whatever you are doing does not lead your feet toward immortality, if your eyes do not open toward immortality, and if your life does not move in the direction where death does not happen, what is the purpose of doing it? How is it meaningful?

Life is an opportunity. Whatever moments we have lost, there is simply no way of getting them back. The opportunity life brings can be used in many ways. Whatever we do with it changes our life accordingly. Some people use it to earn wealth. For their whole life, they use all the opportunities of life, put all their energy, into earning wealth. But when they come face-to-face with death, all their wealth becomes useless. Some people toil their whole life to use this opportunity to attain fame and prestige just so their ego is fulfilled. But when death comes, all their ego, fame, and prestige become futile.

So what is the criterion that your life has not been in vain? The only criterion is that when death confronts you, all that you have earned in life should not be worthless. When you face death, however you have used the opportunity of life – whatever you have staked your whole life on – its meaningfulness should remain intact. Only that which is meaningful in the face of death is truly meaningful; everything else is worthless. I repeat: that which remains meaningful in the face of death, that alone is meaningful and everything else is worthless.

Very few people have this criterion in their minds; very few people have this consideration, this perspective. I would ask you to think over whether you have it or not. Think about this: whatever I accumulate by running my whole life – be it scholarliness or wealth, fasting for austerity, earning fame, writing novels, creating paintings, or singing songs – in the end, in the face of death when my whole life is put to the ultimate test, will these things have any significance or not?

If they won't, it is better to be aware of it this very day. And it is better to move in the direction where you can create such richness, such power, such energy within your being that when you encounter death you will have something within you that is unaffected by death, which even death cannot destroy.

It is possible. And if it weren't possible, all religions would be simply nonsense and futile. It has happened before, it can happen even today. It can happen in everyone's life. But neither does it fall from the sky nor can you get it through charity nor can it be stolen, and it can't be attained for free just by sitting at the feet of some awakened master. Nobody can hand it to you; it can only be given birth by you. It can only be created by your own efforts, by your own life and determination, by putting all your energy into it.

But as long as we feel that what we are doing is perfectly

right, as long as the way we are living seems right to us, we can't take steps in that direction. Somewhere our life is deluded, somewhere it is wrong. We must be aware that our direction in life is taking us on paths which lead nowhere.

The way to give birth to this awareness is to appraise your life as if you are facing death. One day, you will have to appraise it anyway in the face of death, but then there is nothing you can do about it. Someone who starts appraising it beforehand will be able to do something about it. Then something will surely happen in his life, some revolution intensify in his life. So it is essential to start assessing it from today onward, to evaluate it every day.

Bernard Shaw once said that there should be courts in the world where a person has to appear every three years and prove that in those years his life has been meaningful. It was just a joke. Would it be possible to have such courts anywhere? Even if it were, there would be difficulties. How would you prove the meaningfulness of your life? How would you prove, "This is the end result of what I have lived, the significance and meaning"?

Forget it, there are no such courts. But in his mind every person needs to have a court of his own wisdom where he appears every moment. Every day, he should stand in front of it and ask himself, "How am I living? Will something substantial happen by this? Will I gain anything out of it? Will I reach anywhere by it? Will it put an end to my running? Will it eliminate my suffering? Will it dispel darkness? Will it destroy death?"

When all these questions arise with great intensity in someone's mind, religiousness is born in his life. Religiousness is not born by just reading the scriptures, but by constantly appraising your life. You need to appraise it every day; you need to appraise it from moment to moment.

So first I would ask you to think about this. It is the basis for the next three days, when I will talk to you about the path on which we can turn aside from the direction of death, and move in the direction of deathlessness. You too must be thinking that it would be good if your life was immortal. The desire must be arising in your mind that it would be good if you could avoid death. Deep down you must be wondering how you can attain deathlessness.

Unless the totally futility of our present life becomes clear to us, unless all our present ways of living, our patterns, our thought processes, and movements in life are seen as worthless – and we realize that what we are doing is absolutely meaningless – until then an authentic desire to find deathlessness cannot be born in us. As long as there is no restlessness, no nervousness, no anxiety about the meaninglessness of what we are doing, how can the idea, the thought, of going toward the meaningful arise in us?

So today I would like to tell you to confront death face-to-face. All of us keep death hidden. We turn our backs on it, but someone who turns his back on death is living in great delusion.

I was traveling in the rainy season when I had to stop for a while by the side of a mountain river. My car had to stop there because the river was overflowing its banks with great force. There were two or three other cars behind my car and they too had to stop. I didn't know the person in the car behind me, but seeing me sitting alone he came and started a conversation with me. I was just talking casually to him when suddenly he asked me, "What in life is worth thinking about most?"

I told him, "There is only one thing which is worth thinking about and that is death."

We kept talking on many subjects. He told me he would surely meet me on his way back. I told him, "There is no guarantee that we will meet when you come back. Who knows: I may not be alive or you may not be alive, or both of us may be alive yet our paths may not cross."

I told him a short story. I could never have imagined what was going to happen. As the flooding subsided and he was leaving, I told him this story…

An emperor in China became angry with his prime minister. Although the emperor loved him immensely, he imprisoned him and sentenced him to death.

It was the custom in his state that whenever someone was to be hanged, early in the morning on the day of execution the king would personally go and meet him and fulfill his last wish – if he had one.

This was the case with the prime minister whom the king used to love immensely. But he had made a huge mistake which had angered the king, so he punished him with a death sentence. On the day of the hanging, the king came to the prime minister early in the morning. He got down from his horse and told him, "If you have any last wish, I will fulfill it."

The moment he said this, the prime minister had tears in his eyes. The king was astonished. The prime minister was an utterly brave person and had never cried in his life. It was impossible that he would start crying out of fear of death; it was just impossible. The king was really surprised. He said, "I am astonished to see tears in your eyes."

The prime minister said, "I am not crying because my death is fast approaching. I am crying for another reason. I am crying for your horse."

The king asked, "What is there to cry about with my horse?"

The prime minister said, "After toiling for years I have acquired an art. I have learned the science of making a horse fly. Never in my life have I come across a breed of horse which could learn to fly, but the horse you are riding belongs to that breed of horses. That's why I am crying: I have wasted my whole life learning that art because today it will simply die with me."

The king thought that it would be unique if his horse could learn to fly. He said, "Don't be afraid and don't cry. How long will it take for the horse to learn to fly?"

The prime minister said, "Just one year."

The king said, "If the horse can learn to fly, I will cancel your death sentence and you will be reinstated as prime minister. You will be given immense wealth and whatever you want; there is no problem in it. But if the horse does not learn to fly within that year, in a year's time you will be hanged."

The prime minister mounted the horse and returned to his house. There, people were weeping and crying about his death. Seeing him back home everyone was astonished and they asked him, "How come you are back?" He told the whole story. But his wife and children still continued to cry and weep.

He said to them, "Stop crying."

His wife said, "I am sure that you don't know of any art which can make horses fly, so what sort of foolishness is this? If you didn't die today, you will die after a year. But for us, this year will pass waiting for your death. We will anyway be grieving and in sorrow. If you wanted to deceive in this way, you should have asked for at least twenty, or even fifty years."

The prime minister started laughing and said, "You are unacquainted with the laws of life. Who knows what will happen within a year? I may die, the horse may die, or the king may die. One year is a long time. Had I asked for twenty years, the king would not have dared to give them to me. Twenty years would have been too long. So I asked for one year. Anything can happen in this one year: I can die, the horse can die, or the king can die. The matter has been postponed."

And then in the story an incident happened which no one could ever have foreseen: all three of them died within that one year – the king, the prime minister, and also the horse.

Since the flood had subsided he went back to his car. He said to me, "I will definitely see you on my way back."

Again he was saying the same thing. It is such a habit with us that no matter how often someone explains things to us, we again and again start saying and doing the same thing. It happens with me every day. People ask me something and I explain it to them, and then they come and ask something which is totally contrary to what I have said.

So as he was leaving, he again said to me, "I will surely meet you on my return. I am really glad to have met you."

I just laughed. His car left ahead of me. And just after two miles or so down the road I found him lying dead. His car had met with an accident and he had been killed.

My driver said, "This is really strange. Just now you were telling him the same thing."

I tell *you* the same thing. There is no guarantee that when you start for home you will reach it. There is no guarantee and no certainty. Today you may reach it, but tomorrow you may not. Tomorrow you may reach it, but the day after tomorrow you may not. How long can you avoid? A day will surely come when you aren't able to reach. Visualizing that day to be in ten or twenty years' time makes no difference. One who knows this fact will visualize it as being this very night.

Just go from here thinking that tomorrow morning you won't be able to get up – what should you do? Depart from here with this thought: tomorrow morning you won't be there, then what should you do? Someday a morning will surely come when you won't be there. At least this much is certain; there is no reason to doubt it, there is no need to explain it either. There will certainly come a day when the sun will rise, but you won't be there. Many people have been on this earth, but now they are not here anymore. Today you are here, and someday you won't be here.

In life, nothing is more certain than death, but we hardly ever think about it. Everything else is uncertain, everything else is doubtful. It is possible that God may or may not exist; it is possible that the soul may or may not exist. It is also possible that the world we see around us may or may not be there; it may be just a dream. Yet, there is one thing that is certain, one thing that is inevitable and there is not the least doubt about it: someone who is here now will not be here forever. Death will certainly come; there is no greater truth than death.

We never think about our death, we always turn our backs on it. If anyone reminds you about it, you say, "Don't talk about such an ominous thing; don't talk of *any* such things. Why talk about death?" We simply keep the topic of death at a distance, at arm's length. But no matter how far you stay away from death, death loves you immensely and it won't keep away from you for long. Whoever contemplates on life will find that death is the most certain thing.

Why not make this certain fact of life the primary element of contemplation? Why not create a philosophy of life keeping this in mind? Whatever the philosophy of life may be, why should it not be based on the foundation of death? Because this is the only certain foundation, all other foundations are uncertain. Why not have this as the only foundation? It is a fact that has to be faced – if not today then tomorrow – so why not catch hold of it and face it this very day?

The whole direction of life will change for someone who agrees to face it today, for someone who starts contemplating on it today. His life is transformed. The people who are courageous, who are capable of contemplating death, who turn around and face death, who accept death this very day, their feet, their very breath, stop moving in the direction of death. Then a new path and a new door open up in front of them.

I will talk to you about how that path can be opened up. But tonight I only want to share this small thought with you, so that you can think about it and keep it in mind. Tonight, go to sleep thinking about death, so that tomorrow morning when you get up, this thought occurs to you again and again: whatever work you are doing, whatever is happening, whatever you are creating and accumulating, will this have any meaning when in the end you face death?

I am not telling you to renounce work and run away nor am I telling you to stop doing. I am only saying that whatever you are achieving has no meaning, no significance in the presence of death – this much has to become absolutely clear to you. I am not telling you to drop, renounce, everything. I am not telling you to run away. Just this much awareness should become clear to you. Then, on its own accord, a thirst for a new search will begin in your life. You will experience a new thirst. It does not matter that everything continues as it used to be because alongside it a new movement will start. Slowly, slowly you will find that although you are doing the same work as before, your being is no longer involved in that work. Although you are doing the same things, now only your body is involved. Your soul has embraced a totally different direction.

Living in the world means you must maintain the body; these things will still need to be done, but it does not end there. There is something else within you that has to be found and developed – this you will also need to do. But work is not against this. You don't have to drop work because it cannot be found by running away; it is present here. If its direction becomes clear to you and the longing for it becomes clear to you, then even the activities which seem to be futile can become a meaningful part of that greater work.

Earning your living, wearing clothes, or building your home – all these things can become meaningful if your feet start moving in the direction of the soul. All these things will simply become significant in the search for that soul. They will become a background and foundation for it. Then the body becomes a ladder reaching to the soul. In themselves all these things, all these mundane chores, are utterly futile unless your mind starts moving in the direction of the soul. If your being starts moving in that direction, all these things become meaningful. There is no fundamental antagonism between the world and godliness; there is no enmity between godliness and the world. But the world alone is useless. It only becomes meaningful when it starts revolving around the center of godliness.

Mahavira also eats and breathes, Krishna also drinks water, and Christ also wears clothes, but there is a difference, an immense difference. We simply put on clothes, nothing more. We only protect our body, but what for and why? We go on eating food, but what is the purpose of just maintaining the body? We simply go on taking care of the means and then die; there are no ends in our life. Only when there are ends can the means become meaningful. Means in themselves are utterly futile, they simply have no significance.

Let's suppose there is a person who does not want to go anywhere but he starts constructing a road. His whole life he may go on constructing the road. He may break up old roads, destroy the forests to make a path through them, arrange concrete blocks to make the road. If you ask him "Why are you constructing the road?" and he says "I certainly don't want to go anywhere," his building the road has simply been futile. All of us go on building such roads, but we don't want to go anywhere.

For a person who does not want to move toward godliness, life is simply like building a road even though he doesn't want to go anywhere. But if someone's being wants to move toward godliness, toward immortality, all the trivial activities in his life – moving the clay, laying small concrete blocks, destroying the forest to construct a road – become meaningful. All of us construct roads, but very few among us reach because while we are building the roads, the thought of reaching somewhere does not occur to us at all. It is more important to ask oneself why one wants to live rather than just keep on making arrangements for living. Ask why one wants to exist, rather than just go on protecting one's existence.

This thought, this question, should arise in your mind. Very few questions arise in our minds, they simply don't. But if questions don't arise, if there is no inquiry in our minds, how can the search be born? If there is no desire to go on the search, how can you make any effort in that direction?

So in these three days I will by and by talk to you about all this. For tonight, I only want to say that when you go to sleep, sleep with death. As you go to sleep, think that death is sleeping beside you. Keep it constantly near you, next to you. It *is* with you, so keep it next to you. Anyone who keeps death near himself, who makes death his companion and friend, should remember that it won't take long before godliness is with him; he has taken the first step.

Anyone who has made friends with death, has kept it close to him, has already taken the first step. Deathlessness will soon be with him. If not today, then tomorrow. Sooner or later godliness will be with him. The whole secret lies in being close to death. Those who keep death alongside themselves I call seekers. A man who runs away from death, tries to avoid death, does not keep it near him, I call a worldly person.

I won't say more. I will begin my talks tomorrow morning. This is just to create a background. If any meditation can be born in you at all, it can only be born when you have fulfilled this first condition of being a seeker: don't turn away from death.

Look death in the eye, bring it close to you. Tonight, sleep next to it, go to sleep thinking about it, thinking about your own death, thinking that it is close by and can happen at any time, any moment. Tomorrow morning a few more questions may arise in your mind. If they arise, ask me those questions as I will be here for three days to discuss them. If they don't arise, if even after keeping death close to you no thoughts arise, please don't come here again tomorrow morning. It makes no sense, has no meaning. If no thought arises in you when thinking about your own death, don't come here tomorrow morning; it will be meaningless. Whatever I say can only be significant after you have that thought.

If you start seeing your death and this thought and anxiety grips your mind – "Death has surrounded me from all the four sides, what should I do? How can I go beyond it? If everything around me is going to be destroyed, what path should I search for to attain the indestructible?" – only then is your coming here tomorrow meaningful. I am going to talk about the bridge which takes one from death to deathlessness, so only then will what I say be significant for you.

I am grateful to you for listening to me with such love and silence. I pray that godliness may give you the awareness that death is close.

CHAPTER 2

drop borrowed thoughts

My beloved ones.

Last night I talked about death. The search for life can only begin with death. If you want to know life, you have to begin your search with the fact of death; only then will you succeed in finding life. This appears to be contradictory, it looks contradictory: if we want to find life, we have to begin with death – but it is not so. Whoever wants to search for light will have to begin with darkness. The search for light means that we are standing in darkness and light is not available to us. The search for light means that we are in darkness and light is far away, otherwise why we would search for it? So the search for light has to begin with darkness – and the search for life has to begin with death. If we are searching for life, it means we are standing in death. Unless we have a clear awareness of this fact, no further steps can be taken.

Yesterday I primarily told you a few things about death and asked you not to keep death apart from you, but to confront it.

Don't try to avoid death, encounter it. Don't try to run away from death, don't try to forget it; only the constant remembrance of it can be of help to you.

During these three days, I will talk to you in the morning, and in the evening I will discuss your questions. Following on from the discussions we had about death last night, I want to tell you a few things about the topic of the thought-less state. For these three days I have chosen three words for discussion. Today I will talk about the thought-less state, tomorrow I will talk about the state of thinking, and the day after about the state of no-thought.

The thought-less state means a state of mind in which we live blindly and don't think at all; the state of thinking means living consciously and thoughtfully; the state of no-thought means to rise beyond all thoughts and to live in enlightenment. These are the three steps. Today I will talk to you about the thought-less state.

Ordinarily all of us are living in this state – there is no thinking of any kind in our life. Our lives are directed by blind desires, blind lusts, and we have no idea why they are there. Only when we begin to think can an answer to the "why" be found.

We feel hungry, we feel thirsty, desires arise in us and we are engaged in fulfilling them – why? At this level it is simply impossible to give an answer to the why. We feel hungry, so we look for food, but why we feel hungry and why we need to eat is never part of our thinking. Even the most intelligent person feels hungry, but he has no answer for it.

We live just as the whole of nature does – blindly. Rain comes, then the sun shines, the night arrives – why? Why does it rain, why does the sun shine, why does the night arrive? There is no answer to it. A seed sprouts and becomes a tree, it bears leaves, the flowers blossom, and fruit comes – why? There is no answer to it. The animals exist, the birds exist, the insects and the worms exist, human beings also exist – why?

At the level at which we are living, there is no answer. We exist, we have an intense desire to live, so we go on living, but we simply have no answer as to why we exist, and why we have such an intense longing to live. No human being has ever found the answer. This is the level of the thought-less state.

If I abuse you, you become angry. Why do you get angry at someone's abuse? Someone pushes you and violence arises in your mind. Why does it arise? Why do you find someone beautiful? Why do you find someone ugly? You like someone, you dislike someone else. You find someone pleasant, someone else repulsive. You feel like being close to someone, you feel like running away from someone else. Perhaps you have rarely asked yourself why all this happens, and even if you ask you won't get any answer. The question will go on resonating, but no answer can be found.

At the level of the body, at the level of nature, there is no answer. We simply go on living without having any answers. Even when death comes, for that as well no answer can be given. You had no answer as to why you were born, nor can you have an answer as to why you died. You had no answer as to why you were hungry and thirsty, no answer for your desires or for any other instincts, so in the end you cannot have any answer for death either. Just as you have accepted birth, similarly there is no other way but to one day accept death. At this level, answers simply don't exist. This is the level of the body; it is the level of the thought-less state, of instincts – and there no answer exists.

Most people live at this level; they simply live without answers. But a life which has no answer is simply futile. Its meaning is not even visible to oneself.

Recently, a friend of mine committed suicide. He was a thoughtful person; he used to think a lot. Some two months before his death he had come to meet me. For years he had been contemplating death; many times he had thought about committing suicide. He told me, "I want to put an end to my life; I don't see any meaning in it." He had come to ask me for my opinion and advice.

I told him, "If you see some meaning in dying, then certainly put an end to your life. You don't see any meaning in life, but do you see any meaning in death?"

He said, "I don't see any meaning in that either."

I said, "Then it won't make any difference. Even if you put an end to this life, it won't make any difference. The futility will still be present. Life is meaningless and death will also be meaningless, so there is no point in choosing either."

Most people simply go on living, thinking "What will we gain by dying? If we die, what will happen?" So we go on living, but this is certainly not life. Since there is no meaning in opting for death, we go on living.

Two months later he committed suicide. He wrote me a letter before his death in which he wrote, "In the end I have simply decided to put to an end to my life."

In the last fifty years, many people have put an end to their lives, people who had no suffering and no pain or anguish of any sort, who had no financial problems at all. But they committed suicide only for this reason: they could not find any meaning in life. If you also think, if you also contemplate and ponder, perhaps you will also find hardly any reason to live. And if you have no answer to why you should live, neither your life can have any depth nor can it have any experience. Your living or not living are almost the same. If you are there, it is fine, and if you are not there, that too is fine.

As I see it, at the level of the body, no answer to life can be found – and all of us live only at the level of the body. We live just because we feel hungry, we feel thirsty, we need clothes, we need a house. Just think for a while: what will you do if you get all these things? If your hunger is satisfied, if your thirst is quenched, if all your desires are fulfilled, you get everything you want, you won't have any other choice but to die. If all your desires are fulfilled, what will you do? Will you then be able to live for even a single moment longer? You will sleep, you will endlessly sleep. Even now, as long as your desires keep you running, you run. But when you have no other activity, you have nothing to do except sleep. If all your wishes are fulfilled, you won't have anything else to do except die.

At the level of the body there are problems, and we simply live to solve them. But always be aware that because the body has been born it will die. That which has been born will die, that which has begun will come to an end. The life that exists at the level of the body will inevitably take you to death. There are no two opinions about it, nor can there be. Can there be another life beyond this? As far as the level of the body is concerned, no meaning has been found. But can some meaning be found at another level?

The body is an utterly fixed machine of nature. Just as nature functions mechanically, similarly the body functions. There, there is no freedom; there, everything is dependent. Mahavira's body was dependent, Krishna's and Christ's bodies were also dependent – yours and mine as well – because Mahavira died, Krishna and Christ also died.

As far as the level of the body is concerned, until now no one has become independent and no one has found immortal life: no one has ever found it and no one will ever be able to find it. The body is mortal, there is no immortality there. The body is the abode of death; there is no life there. If we simply go on revolving in the same circle, then – as I told you last night – no matter what we do we will move toward death.

The body is utterly dependent, there is no freedom there. Is there anything within us which is beyond the body, which transcends the body? Certainly: the mind – and we get a few glimpses of it. Every man is aware that he has a mind. He can hear the footsteps of his thoughts. When thoughts arise in contemplation he gets some indication that the mind exists.

The body is, as I said, unavoidably dependent, but the mind isn't. The mind *can* become independent, but ordinarily the mind is also dependent. At the level of the mind too there is no freedom in our life. At the level of the mind, we are also dependent. At the level of the body, desires and instincts have gripped us. At the level of mind, we are gripped by beliefs; at the level of mind, words, scriptures, doctrines have caught hold of us. The mind is also a slave. The mind walks and moves on the path of dependency; there is no freedom there.

But mind can become independent. That is the difference between the body and the mind. The body is dependent and cannot become independent; the mind is also dependent, but it can become independent. And there is an element beyond all this which is called the soul – you can also give it other names. I will talk about it; we will work toward it. The soul is independent and it cannot be dependent. These are the three levels of life: the body which is dependent and cannot become independent; the mind which is dependent, but can become independent; the soul which is independent and is incapable of becoming dependent.

Only a mind that is independent is capable of knowing the soul – which without doubt is free and alive, which is immortal, which knows no birth and no death. If the mind is dependent, it won't be able to know anything other than the body. A dependent mind cannot look beyond the dependent body. As long as our mind is dependent, we will feel that we are nothing other than the body. But if the mind is independent, it will raise its eyes toward the soul that is free, alive.

Therefore it is neither a question of the body nor of the soul. While meditating, the whole question is centered around the mind: are our minds independent or are they dependent? If the mind is dependent, life cannot rise beyond the body. Then life will take you to death. But if the mind is independent, then life's eyes can begin to look toward immortality.

Ordinarily our minds are dependent. Our minds have not known any freedom. Not only do we wear the same clothes as others, not only do we eat what others eat, we also think what others think. At the level of thinking too we are followers – and someone who is a follower is dependent. Anyone who follows another is dependent. So at the level of the body we are dependent, and at the level of the mind we have also made ourselves dependent. Have you ever had one or two thoughts of your own, or are all your thoughts borrowed? Has a single thought ever been born inside you, or have you gathered all your thoughts from the outside?

You may have many thoughts in your mind, so just watch them a little. If you watch, you will find that they have come from somewhere and have accumulated inside you. Just as the birds come and sit on the trees in the evening, similarly the thoughts have come and inhabited our minds. They are all others' thoughts; they are aliens, borrowed. Only someone who is able to generate one or two thoughts of his own has the right to call himself a man. Then inside him freedom begins; otherwise we are dependent.

All human beings are dependent and the root of their dependency is that they have never thought anything of their own. They have simply accepted all those alien thoughts; they have said yes to them. They have developed faith in them; they have developed trust in them, have started believing them. For thousands of years, people have been taught to believe and not to think. People have been taught to have faith and not to contemplate. For thousands of years, people have been taught blind trust and not to contemplate. For thousands of years, conviction, faith, and belief have been taught, but not contemplation. And the outcome of all this is that mankind has constantly become more and more dependent. Our minds have been tied in chains. They simply repeat things borrowed from others, they don't think anything of their own.

Whatever question I ask, your answer will be almost a repetition; it won't come out of your contemplation. If I ask you "Does God exist?" just think whether the answer that comes from within is really yours. If I ask you "Is there a soul?" just think whether the answer coming from within – "Yes, there is a soul"; "No, there is no soul" – has arisen out of your thinking or has simply come from your background. Have you read it in some scripture? Have you heard it from some master and accepted it? Or have you known it? If the answer is not coming out of your knowing, know well that your mind is dependent.

Forget about the soul and God, even the most normal experiences of life are not our own; those we also repeat. If I show you a roseflower and ask you whether it is beautiful, you will perhaps say "Yes, it is beautiful." But contemplate a little on this: have you simply accepted it or have you yourself known it? Different races in the world consider different kinds of flowers to be beautiful; different communities in the world consider different faces to be beautiful. Children born in a certain community simply learn its definition of beauty, and go on repeating it their whole lives.

A nose which is considered beautiful in India is not considered beautiful in China. Then a doubt arises whether this experience of beauty is our own or has been acquired from society. A face which is considered beautiful in India is not considered beautiful in Japan, and the face of a Negro person – considered beautiful in a Negro community – will not be considered beautiful in India. In India, thin lips are considered beautiful, but for a Negro, fuller lips are beautiful. Now a Negro child will go on repeating his whole life that full lips are beautiful, whereas a child born in India will go on repeating his whole life that thin lips are beautiful. Which lips are beautiful? Which face, which flower? This is not our own experience; we are only repeating.

If I ask you what love is, you will only repeat some answer. You must have read about it in some scripture. You may hardly have known and explored love. If our personality and mind are so repetitive, if they simply echo society, they won't be independent – how can they be? We are only echoes, we are only repetition. Society's voice goes on echoing through us and we go on repeating it. We are not individuals; individuality has simply not been born in us.

How can a person in whom individuality has not been born attain immortality? What do you have that you want to preserve? What do you have that you can say is yours, that you can say you have known and lived? If you don't have anything, then death is certain and all that you have acquired from society will be useless. What have you created that you have not acquired from society, that has not come from someone else? Can you say what is authentically yours? If you don't have anything, how will you be able to see your inner soul?

When you have something authentically your own in your mind, you start moving toward the soul. Then you become worthy, then you are able to know the soul. Until you have an independent mind, it is simply impossible for individuality to be born. Our minds are utterly dependent; our minds are slaves. And mind's slavery is very deep.

In a thousand and one ways we have been prepared for slavery. In every way there are efforts to make us a slave – and there are reasons for these efforts. It is in the interest of society that a person remains a slave, it is in the interest of the state that a person remains a slave, it is in the interest of the religions and the sects that a person remains a slave, and in the interest of the priests and pundits. The more enslaved a person is, the more he can be exploited. The more enslaved a person is, the less possibility for him to revolt. If a person's mind is completely dependent, he is no danger to society. Revolt and revolution become impossible.

Society doesn't want anyone's mind to be independent. Hence right from childhood, society tries in every way to make a person dependent. The foundation for making someone's mind a slave is education and conditioning. Before we realize it, we are already tied in chains. The chains have many names – it could be Hindu, it could be Jaina, it could be Indian or non-Indian, it could be Christian or Mohammedan: the chains have different labels, different names on them. A thousand and one chains fetter our minds, and sooner or later we stop noticing them.

Very few people think, most people simply quote. Then it makes no difference whether they quote Mahavira, whether they quote Buddha, whether they quote the Gita or the Koran. As long as you quote someone, you commit the greatest sin to your soul. As long as you quote someone, you are not willing to be independent. Society says: those who don't have faith will not find the soul; those who don't believe won't be able to find *moksha*. But this is so foolish!

Belief is blind, belief is bondage, but *moksha* is ultimate freedom. How can you find *moksha* through belief? How can you find the soul through belief? Belief is simply blind. It is blind on the same level as the blindness of the body: the blindness of desire. If this same level of blindness is born in the mind, it becomes belief. I ask you to drop all beliefs and give birth to thinking. A state of belief is a thought-less state.

But why do we start believing in the first place? One can understand that believing is in the interest of the society, believing is in the interest of exploitation, believing is in the interest of the temples and the priests: their whole business depends on belief. The day you stop believing, that very day, their whole business will collapse. So one can certainly understand that it is in their interest, but why does anyone *start* believing? Why do you and I start believing?

We start believing because belief is available without making any effort, without hard work, whereas thinking is an effort. To think, you will have to go through pain, anxiety; to think, you will have to go through suffering. To think, you will have to doubt, you will have be confused. In thinking you are alone, whereas in belief the whole crowd is with you. In belief there is a kind of security, a kind of support, but in thinking there is great insecurity. There is fear of going astray, there is a possibility of committing mistakes, and there is fear of disappearing.

So in the world of belief we walk with the crowd. When thousands of people are walking along that highway we don't feel afraid – all around us there are so many people. The path of belief is simply the path of the crowd; the path of thinking is the path of aloneness. There you will be alone, there you will not have any support because you will not have any crowd around you. A crowd can make you believe in things that you hadn't even imagined.

Aristotle wrote that women have fewer teeth than men. In the West, this man is considered to be very intelligent, he is considered to be the father of logic, the pioneer of logic. He did not have just one wife, he had two, but he never bothered to open his wife's mouth and count how many teeth she had. For thousands of years it was believed in Greece that women have fewer teeth than men. In fact, women are supposed to have less of everything than men because a woman is supposed to be a lower kind of animal. Man is a higher kind, so how can a woman have an equal number of teeth? It was obvious, so no one bothered to count them.

Women are in such a pitiable state that they simply accept whatever the men say. They have never counted their own teeth! So if a man – Aristotle – wrote in a book that women have fewer teeth than men, in Europe, thousands of years after his death, it was believed. But the thought never occurred to any intelligent person that he should count them. The thought of counting can only occur to someone who starts thinking. If someone just believes, there is just no question of counting.

For thousands of years, the crowd has believed in a thousand and one idiocies. There are many intelligent people in the crowd, but thinking never occurs to them because doubt never arises in their minds. If doubt doesn't arise in someone's mind, thinking cannot be born. There is no greater spiritual ability than to doubt. There is no greater sin than to have faith and there is no greater religion than to doubt. One has to doubt, because if doubt does not arise, you cannot get rid of the society and the crowd. You cannot become independent. The crowd simply tells you not to doubt because anyone who doubts will be destroyed.

But I say to you that someone who doubts has found, and someone who believes is destroyed – there is no question about it. He was already destroyed the moment he started believing. Belief means "I am blind and I accept whatever is being said." Doubt means "I am not willing to be blind, I will think. Until and unless I experience it myself, I am not ready to believe." In doubt there is courage and in belief there is laziness. It is due to laziness that we have started believing. Who wants to go on a search? So whatever others say, we simply believe it.

When a tradition survives for thousands of years it is powerful. We think that people cannot have been wrong for thousands of years: if all that time billions and billions of people have been thinking along these lines, then surely they must be right. The crowd sanctions what the truth about something is, but the crowd is never proof of authenticity. Quite often the crowd simply goes on imitating those who have died, the crowd never experiences: there is no way that a crowd can experience anything.

An individual experiences, but the society cannot experience. The society does not have a soul that can experience; the society is simply a dead machine. Hence someone who remains dependent on the society, slowly, slowly he too becomes a machine, his individuality is destroyed. No one can become religious without having freed himself of the society.

You must have heard about sannyasins escaping from, renouncing, the society – but they don't renounce. They renounce their home and their family, but no sannyasin renounces the society. If a sannyasin truly renounces the society, he certainly attains truth. Even after becoming a sannyasin, someone born into the Jaina religion says "I am a *Jaina* monk" – this shows that he has not renounced the society. He has renounced his home, but has not renounced the society; he has renounced his wife, but he has not renounced his religious leaders. Although he has escaped at the level of the body, at the level of mind he is still a slave.

There is no point in escaping at the level of the body. The real question is of escaping at the level of the mind. His mind is still in the grip of the religion which he has been taught and trained in right from childhood. Whatever answers he has been given, they are still sitting in his mind. He still repeats the scriptures he has been taught. At the level of the mind, he is a slave.

I tell you not to escape at the level of the body. No one can escape at the body level. Even if a sannyasin thinks he has escaped at the body level, he has not really escaped because he has to come back to the society to ask for food, he has to come back to the society to ask for clothes. At the level of the body, how can one run away from the society?

He could have become free at the level of the mind. But as he could not become free at that level, he has fallen into the arrogance of becoming free at a level where no one can become free. At the level of the body, no one can simply run away. At the level of body, you have to live among the group. Even the greatest saint has to live with the support of the group. But he could have become free at the level of the mind – that is where you have to become free. But he could not.

So I don't tell you that you should renounce the home and family, all that is simply madness. But if someone can drop the walls of the home of the mind, if he can break down the rooms he has created in his mind, if he can destroy the chains, freedom will begin in his life.

So the first thing is: doubt. Doubt whatever you have been taught. Not because it is wrong; please understand this correctly. Doubt Mahavira, doubt Buddha, not because what Buddha and Mahavira say is wrong – not because of that. No, it is because it is wrong to believe. Understand this. Doubt the Koran, doubt the Bible and doubt the Gita, not because what is written in them in wrong; I am not saying that. What I am saying is that it is wrong to believe and if you believe in it, you will never be able to know that which is written and said. But if you doubt, one day the same truth will be revealed to you which has been revealed to Mahavira or Buddha.

Doubt destroys the thought-less state; belief intensifies the thought-less state. Belief is the supporter of the thought-less state and doubt destroys the thought-less state.

But in thinking, there will certainly be pain. Thinking is austerity. Fasting is not austerity. Being hungry is not great austerity, being thirsty is not great austerity: they even do it in a circus. But to doubt is immense austerity. To doubt means to be ready to stand in insecurity, to be ready to stand in ignorance, to be ready to stand on one's own feet and to drop all crutches. And remember: as long as someone walks with crutches, his feet will never be strong enough to walk on their own.

As long as someone believes, his mind cannot gather enough strength to find the truth. It is only when we are insecure that we gather the strength. It is only in insecurity that our energy accumulates, that it awakens. If I tell you to run, you will run, but very slowly. If I tell you to run with all your strength and energy, even then you will run quite slowly. But if someone is pointing a gun at you, threatening your life, your feet will gain such a momentum which even you yourself never imagined was possible.

Once it happened…

In Japan, a servant of a great emperor fell in love with the queen. The moment the emperor came to know this… It was utterly indecent and humiliating that an ordinary servant, a slave, should fall in love with the queen and she with him. Society has its own standards, but love does not know who is a slave, who is a servant: love knows nothing of king and servant. Love simply makes whoever falls in love a king, and he who does not fall in love remains a nobody.

The king thought, "What kind of mess is this? It is very humiliating and when this rumor spreads, it will be awful." He called the servant.

The servant was a truly lovable man and the king used to love him immensely. He told the servant, "It would have been appropriate for me to take a sword and cut off your head. But I have loved you, you have been a unique person, so I will give you one chance. Take a sword and stand opposite me. Let us fight each other. Whoever dies, dies; whoever survives will become the queen's husband."

This was very compassionate on the part of the king because it was not at all necessary for him to fight with the servant and give him a chance. He could just have killed him.

The servant said, "What you say is fair, but the matter ends there and then because I have never used a sword in my life. So if I now take one up, how long will I be able to fight you? And you are so skilled. Your fame as a swordsman is spread far and wide; there is no greater swordsman than you. Although you say that you are being compassionate to me, this is surely not compassion. I know what it means, I know what the end result is going to be. I have never held a sword in my hands, I don't even know *how* to hold a sword. How will I win against you?"

But since it was the king's order, he had to take the sword. All the courtiers were standing nearby watching the fight. The king had won many battles in his life. It was well known that there was no swordsman more skilled than him. But when they started fighting, the people were astonished and the king himself was astonished: it was difficult for the king to use his swordsmanship against the servant. The servant certainly did not know anything of swordsmanship, but time and time again the king had to retreat. The servant was attacking him so severely that he became afraid. The attacks were totally unskilled, totally chaotic; they were outside the technique of swordsmanship.

The servant had only one option: to kill or be killed, so he gathered all his energy. All his dormant energy was awakened as there was no alternative: the king had decided that he would die, so now he was doing anything and everything to kill the king.

In the end the king shouted at him to stop. The king said, "I am amazed, I have never seen such a man in my life. I have fought many wars, but how can an ordinary servant attain such strength and energy?"

His old prime minister said, "I knew beforehand that today you would be in trouble. You are a skilled swordsman, so for you there was no question of death. But for the servant, although he is not skilled, it was a question of life or death. So your energies were not completely awake whereas all his energies *had* to be completely awake. That's why it was impossible to win against him."

It is only when man loses all his crutches that his inner energies are awakened. As long as we cling to supports, we are our own enemies and we don't allow the dormant energies within us to awaken. Belief is suicidal because belief does not allow your wisdom and your thinking to become awake. There is no need for them to awaken, there is no opportunity.

But what will happen if you discard all beliefs? You will be compelled to think, every moment you will be forced to think. Then every single issue – even the smallest – will become an opportunity for you to think. You will have to think because it will simply be impossible for you to survive without thinking. Discard all beliefs. Then the dormant energy of thinking within you will have a unique awakening. Only someone who discards all beliefs attains wisdom.

The people who have attained wisdom up to now have only attained it after discarding all beliefs. We cannot attain wisdom because we cling to beliefs. We cling to beliefs out of laziness, out of fear. We cling to beliefs thinking: "What will happen if there are no crutches? Without crutches we will fall." But I say to you that it is better to fall rather than to rely on any support, because when you fall you are at least doing something: you are falling. At least something is happening of your own doing. Even though it is only falling, it is your doing. And if you fall, you will certainly do something to get up again – who wants to keep lying down?

But when you are leaning, standing, on some support, it is not your own doing. You are not standing on your own; someone is supporting you. That kind of standing is utterly pseudo; it is fake. Falling down is real; leaning on someone's shoulders for support, standing supported on someone's shoulders, is fake. Drop all supports. If you really want to discover life, drop all supports. Discard all beliefs. Give thinking the chance, the power, to be active, to work. Give thinking the chance to be born within you.

If you want to learn swimming, it is enough to simply jump into the water without any support. The people who know something about this, who teach people to swim, do only one thing: they simply push you into the water. Everyone has a deep desire to save himself and that alone becomes swimming. But if someone thinks that he won't even enter the water without having first learned how to swim, he better know that he will never be able to learn it. Someday he will have to enter the water without knowing how to swim. Someday he will have to jump into the unknown and unfamiliar water because only by doing that will the ability to swim be awakened in him.

But the mind constantly hankers for supports. A mind that is seeking supports is seeking slavery. Whatever support we seek, we simply become its slave; we become the slave of the one whose support we seek. He may be a master or he may be a god; he may be an avatar or he may be a *tirthankara* – or someone else. Who-ever's support we seek, we become his slave. If you drop all sup-ports, that which is present within you will awaken; the energy that is lying hidden within you will rise. It will awaken with great intensity.

If you decide to be independent at the level of mind, no one in the world can deprive you of knowing your soul. But you will have to make a decision: "Now I decide to become independent at the level of the mind. I decide that I won't accept anyone's slavery at the level of my thinking. I decide that I won't become anyone's follower. No scriptures and no doctrines will be able to burden my mind. I will only consider that truth to be truth which I find for myself. Someone else may have another truth, but it is not truth for me."

If you do not have this much courage, you cannot find life. If you do not have this much courage, your mind may never become independent.

Let me also tell you this: a slavery that lasts a long time becomes appealing; a slavery that lasts a long time starts appear-ing pleasant. You feel afraid of breaking free from it, you feel afraid to leave it. The greatest obstacle to removing slavery is that the slave himself falls in love with his slavery – nobody else can free him. The slave himself starts loving his slavery to the extent that he is even ready to die to defend it. Slaves have given their lives just to protect their slavery. It has been happening all over the world, for thousands of years.

During the French revolution, revolutionaries broke into the Bastille. People had been imprisoned there for hundreds of years. It was the oldest prison in France and they imprisoned the most heinous criminals there, prisoners who had been sentenced to life imprisonment. Some prisoners had been imprisoned there for thirty years, some for forty years and some for fifty years. So the revolutionaries thought that when they break open the prison, how happy the prisoners will feel upon being released.

They went and broke open the prison and released the prisoners from the dark cells. Their hands and feet had been chained for years. Some had been chained for the last forty years, some for the last thirty years and some for at least fifty years. Someone had been imprisoned at the age of twenty, now he was eighty years old; he had spent sixty years fettered in chains. So they broke the prisoners' chains and told them, "Go. Now you all are independent, now you all are free."

But the prisoners were stunned and said, "No, we are fine here. We will feel terrible outside. We have spent sixty years of our life in these dark cells. We have even started liking them; they have become our home. We are afraid to go outside, what will we do there? Who will give us food, who will give us water? Now we don't have any friends or loved ones outside."

But the revolutionaries were stubborn and that day they forcibly brought them up from the cells. The next day they were released. When they were brought up from the cells, but still inside the prison, they were crying, saying that they didn't even want to be there. And when they were released, told they could leave, they were even more upset because they didn't want to go outside. By the evening, half the prisoners had returned to the prison.

This is a unique incident in history.

Those prisoners said, "Forgive us, we were absolutely fine here. We don't feel good outside. Without the chains we feel naked. Without the chains we feel as if our body has lost weight. We don't feel good without them."

At the level of the body there are chains and at the level of mind there are also chains – and we simply don't feel good without them. If I tell you not to be a Hindu for a while, you will start feeling very uneasy, you will become very restless. If I tell you to stop being a Hindu or a Jaina, a Mohammedan or a Christian –

as these are all slaveries – and to start being just a man, you will become very restless and you will feel: "Without being a Hindu, how can I exist? How can I exist without being a Mohammedan? How can I exist unless I am attached to some sect? I will be utterly empty. I will be in great difficulty." For thousands of years you have remained in invisible chains, and they have taken hold of your mind.

Just think a little, contemplate a little, gather a little courage, and gather some resolve. You need to have resolve if you want to go on a search for religion, a search for truth. If someday you want to find that which changed Gautam Siddhartha into Buddha, Jesus into Christ and Mahavira into Jina, if you really you want to find that, then remember: all chains are fatal, are a hindrance.

Nietzsche has written that the first and last Christian was crucified, died on the cross – the first and the last. He wrote it about Christ. So if the first and the last Christian died on the cross, what about the "Christians" who came after him? Who are these Christians? What's it all about? The Christians who came after him cannot become Jesus because to become Jesus you need to have individuality, be free in every way. They are simply the slaves of Jesus.

A follower of Mahavira can never become Mahavira because to become Mahavira your soul has to be independent in every way. He is simply a slave of Mahavira. A person who follows Buddha can never become Buddha. In fact, those who only follow can never become anybody, because those who follow are in trouble, have committed a fundamental mistake: the moment they started following someone they started losing their souls. They have sold their freedom and accepted slavery.

So this morning I want to tell you that in the thought-less state, faiths and beliefs do not allow man's mind to become independent; they keep it dependent. A dependent mind can know only the body; it cannot know anything beyond it. If the mind becomes independent, it can know that which is the source of ultimate freedom – call it the soul, God or any other name. Only an independent mind can become capable of knowing freedom. Only an independent mind can look toward an independent soul. A dependent mind is only capable of looking at the dependent body.

So, as I have said, the body is unavoidably dependent and the soul in unavoidably independent. The mind can be independent as well as dependent. It is in your hands which your mind is – independent or dependent. If you want to keep your mind only dependent, you won't be able to know anything beyond the body. As the body will die, you won't be able to know anything beyond death. But if your mind becomes independent, the soul can be known. The soul is immortal; it has neither birth nor death. However, it cannot happen just by my saying so. If I say that the soul is neither born nor dies and you just repeat it, it is dangerous, it has become a belief.

So I say to you: don't just believe that the soul exists. As of now, don't believe this. Right now you only need to know that your mind is dependent, and you have to fill yourself with the longing to make it independent. The day your mind becomes independent, that very day you will start getting a glimpse of the inner soul. The day your mind becomes completely independent, that day you will become rooted in the soul. That alone is life; that alone is immortality. That alone is the center of the whole world, of all power, and of the whole of existence. There alone is hidden the meaning of life. But only those who are willing to be independent can know that meaning. If you want to know the truth of life, first you must be free. If you are ready for it, the truth of life can be known. If you are not ready, there is no way to know anything other than death.

I have said a few things about the thought-less state, about belief. Tomorrow I will talk about how our minds can become independent. Tomorrow I will talk about the thinking state and the day after about the state of no-thought.

The thinking state is just a ladder. You should not stop there; you have to go beyond it. When we have to climb onto a roof, we use a ladder, but if we stop at the ladder, we cannot reach the roof. So we use the ladder and then we discard the ladder. In order to reach the soul, we will have to go from the thought-less state to the thinking state; and we will have to drop the thinking state and attain a state of no-thought. The day after tomorrow I will talk about the state of no-thought.

Whatever questions you have about this… You should have many questions because I have been telling you to doubt. If you doubt what I say, questions will arise in you. Only if you doubt will the questions arise. Doubt immensely, as much as you can, doubt to the ultimate. The more you doubt, the more will thinking awaken within you. So don't just believe blindly what I have said. Don't accept it – doubt it. Doubt whatever I have said: raise questions, think, and contemplate.

I am not here to give you any teaching. There cannot be a more dangerous thing than a teaching. I am not here to teach; I am not a teacher. I am simply here to awaken something within you. I can give you a push, but no teaching. I can give you a shock, but no teaching. Perhaps your sleep may end after that shock. Someone may wake up, may become disturbed from within, may become restless – and something may arise in him.

After I woke up this morning, a friend came to me and said, "The whole night I kept thinking about death and I could not sleep after that. I became restless, felt disturbed. What you say is certainly right: if death is going to happen, whatever I am doing is futile. Then should I become inactive? Should I stop all activity?"

I was very happy that he could not sleep the whole night. If sleep disappears from your life, it will be the greatest gratitude to existence. If you can become that anxious, if that much doubt arises in you, if that much thinking awakens within you that you cannot sleep, something can happen in your life. But just now you are sleeping in such a relaxed way that there is not the least possibility of anything happening in your life.

I will conclude this talk with a short story…

The mystic Bheekhan was visiting a village and one evening he gave a discourse. While he was talking, a man was sleeping right in front of him. Perhaps his name was Asoji. Bheekhan interrupted his talk in the middle and asked him, "Asoji, are you sleeping?"

He immediately opened his eyes and said, "No, no, what do you mean? Me, sleeping?"

Anyone who sleeps like this never accepts that he is sleeping. So although he *was* sleeping, he immediately opened his eyes and said, "No, I am not sleeping."

Again the discourse started, but how long can a sleepy person stay awake? He went off to sleep again. Once more Bheekhan asked him, "Asoji, are you sleeping?"

He replied, "No," and again opened his eyes. This time he said no more loudly than before, because if he said it softly people might become suspicious. So this time he said more loudly, "I am not sleeping at all. Why are you asking me again and again whether I am sleeping?"

The village people were also listening to the conversation and if they came to know that Asoji was sleeping during the discourse, it would harm his reputation. But this didn't seem to matter. The discourse continued, and after a while he again fell asleep!

What Bheekhan then asked him was something really unique. He asked, "Asoji, are you living?"

Asoji answered, "No," because in his sleep he heard Bheekhan again asking him the same thing: whether he is sleeping. "Not at all."

Bheekhan said, "Now you have answered honestly."

A person who remains asleep does not live. No matter how

often he says, "No, no, I am not sleeping," it has no value. It is not a question of being answerable to anyone, it is only a question of looking inside oneself and contemplating, "Am I sleeping in life? Do I continue to sleep? No questions are arising within me. No anxiety is arising, no restlessness about life. Nor is any discontentment, any disturbance, arising."

People must have told you that a religious person is calm and contended. But I don't tell you that. A religious person is utterly discontented with his life, he is utterly disturbed. Nowhere in his life does he find peace. His whole life looks futile to him. A deep pain, a deep anguish, is born inside him. His whole being starts trembling; his whole being is filled with anxiety. Out of that anxiety, out of that thinking and contemplation, a new direction begins; he starts on a new search.

Blessed are those who are discontented. Those who are contented are almost dead. Now there is simply no opportunity for anything to happen inside them.

So I don't want to give you any teaching. I want to give you discontentment. Many of you must have come here with the idea of attaining peace, silence. I want to make you disturbed because those who cannot get totally disturbed will simply never be able to find peace. For someone who cannot be thoroughly discontented, contentment is not his destiny.

May existence make you discontented, may your sleep get disturbed and everything start appearing futile to you. May whatever you are doing not look right to you. May the path you are walking on not look like the right path. If you find that your friends are not friends, your companions are not companions, and that all the supports in your life are collapsing – you stand utterly helpless and insecure – thinking can be born in you.

Whatever questions there are about this, we will discuss this evening.

CHAPTER 3

faith and belief hinder freedom

Many questions have come to me. Most of the questions have arisen out of our discussion in the morning session where I asked you to start thinking independently.

Someone has asked…

> Osho,
> If there is no faith, what will happen to the
> common man?

People are very much concerned about the common man. This morning, as I finished my talk, someone else came and asked me, "What will happen to the common man? Will he not simply go astray?" – as if right now the common man has not gone astray; as if right now the common man is fine as he is! It is simply accepted that the common man's condition is just fine as it is, in an utterly fine condition. But that if his faith is shaken, if he discards beliefs, he will go astray.

He has also asked…

> Osho,
> If one drops faith and trust, if there were no faith or
> belief, would it not lead to degradation and to the
> spread of misbehavior?

As if right now there is immensely good conduct, as if right now great ethics are being spread, as if for thousands of years there has been no misbehavior.

If the situation we are in right now is not that of misbehavior, what is what then is misbehavior? What do we have in life which we can say is not a downfall? But since it has been going on for thousands of years, we have become accustomed to it. And if we deviate from that as well, we will feel very afraid. It is like a sick person who asks, "If I take some medicine and my sickness is cured, what will happen?"

The outcome of having faith and belief is that man has fallen. The very foundation of that downfall is blindness; the downfall begins with blindness. For a person who has borrowed his thinking and contemplation, what else can happen in his life other than downfall? Someone who has destroyed his own dignity, who has simply destroyed his freedom to think, cannot be in a better condition than the animals. If there is any difference at all between animals and man, then it is only that man is capable of thinking. If we stop thinking and start believing, we inevitably fall into the state of an animal. For someone who does not think, there remains no other way but to fall. It is this whole propaganda of thousands of years of faith and belief which has brought us to this state.

To ask such a question – "Will an ordinary man go astray?" – means only one thing: whoever is asking it considers himself to be an extraordinary person. Anyone who asks this, asks it out of pity for others. He feels that he himself has nothing to fear as he is utterly special, only others – ordinary people – will go astray!

Lately I have had the chance to meet thousands of people every day, and until now I have not met a single person who might have said "I am an ordinary man." Every single person is under the delusion that he is special and everyone else is ordinary. Everyone asks me the same question: "What will happen to the ordinary people?" Until now, not a single person has come and asked me: "What will happen to *me*?"

Where are these common people? I have also been searching for them, but I have not found them yet. If you find them, please let me know who they are. Who are these common people? And who are the chosen few? It is only the ego which considers itself to be special and others to be ordinary. And each and every person has this ego: he is special and all the rest are the common people.

In Arabia there is an old proverb which says that whenever God creates a person and sends him into the world, he whispers a strange thing into his ears. When he creates him, is about to send him into the world, he tells him, "I have never created a better person than you." He tells this to everyone. And it seems to be true. Something of this sort must be happening, otherwise each and every person could not be so deluded.

Gandhi went to England to participate in a conference in London. His secretary, Mahadev Desai, went to meet George Bernard Shaw. Mahadev said to him, "You must also consider Gandhi to be a mahatma, a virtuous soul, don't you?"

Bernard Shaw said, "I do, but I consider him to be the number two. As far as the number one is concerned, that's me!"

Mahadev was very shocked. He had never thought this could happen. In India no one would dare to say that he is the number one. Someone may think it deep down in his heart, but he would not say it openly. It might be said behind someone's back, but no one would say it in front of him. So Mahadev could never have imagined that anyone would tell him straight out that Gandhi is the number two virtuous soul and he is the number one. He came back feeling utterly dejected and related this to Gandhi.

Gandhi said, "It seems that Shaw is a very authentic, honest, man. He has only said what every person feels about himself."

Everyone lives under the delusion that he is extraordinary and the rest are ordinary. Hence everyone is concerned about the rest – the ordinary people. What will happen to them? What will happen to those poor fellows? So let me tell you that this kind of ego is very ordinary. The thought "I am special" is a sign of a most ordinary man. It never occurs to those who are truly special that they are special. Those who are really special never think they are special. At the same time, they don't think that anyone is ordinary.

If you ask me whom I would call an ordinary person, I can only say that an ordinary person is one who does not believe in his own intelligence, in his own thinking, but instead believes in another person's intelligence and thinking. Only such a person is ordinary. If he wants to break out of the confinement of being called ordinary, the first thing he will have to do is drop the blindness of faith and belief.

When I say to you that you will have to drop the blindness of having faiths and beliefs, it means you will have to believe in yourself. A person who believes in others inevitably disbelieves in himself. It is the distrust in oneself that becomes the trust in others. If I don't believe in my own strength, then I will believe in the strength of other people. And if I have trust in my own strength, I will *not* believe in the strength of other people.

Believing in oneself is no hindrance, but believing in another is fatal. When I told you to think, it was in the sense of self-belief. When I tell you to stand on your own feet, to think and contemplate on your own, to experience on your own, I am telling you to believe in yourself. I purposely did not use the word *belief* because that word has become poisonous and can create delusion. Hence I told you to think, I told you to investigate on your own. But my purpose is very clear. My purpose is: I want you to stop believing in others and start believing in yourself. Believing in the self is the only path toward the soul. When I insist that you stop believing in others it is only for one reason: you can start believing in yourself.

No one is ordinary. Only a person who does not believe in himself is ordinary, he alone is sick. What *will* happen to the common man if he starts believing in himself? Whatever happens, it will be very positive. What is the fear behind this question? There are reasons for this fear.

One reason is, we are afraid that the common man will become a man of free will, he will become immoral, he will become unethical, he will drop morality, he will drop spirituality. But why this fear? We have this fear because today whatever spirituality we see in people has been forcibly imposed on them. Whatever morality we see in them, they have been burdened with. If they get a chance to become independent, the first thing they will do is immediately drop this burden. That is the fear.

If freedom takes away our morality and our spirituality, we should know that those moralities and spiritualities must be fake. A morality or a spirituality that is taken away from us by the birth of freedom is certainly fake. Only those spiritualities and moralities which become deeper and more profound by the birth of freedom are authentic. But because our spirituality is fake, our morality and ethics are phony, we have this fear.

The spirituality which has been imposed on man is fake, his whole morality is false. His good conduct has not arisen out of his soul but rather, due to some fear and greed, he wears it like a cloak. Hence the fear that if man starts thinking independently he will become immoral. This fear is indicative of one thing: even now man must be immoral.

Freedom is simply a test. You don't steal, because a policeman is standing on the road; you don't steal, because a magistrate is sitting in the court. Then there is also the court of God which will send you to hell and heaven: that's why you don't steal. If all these courts disappear, if all authority disappears – right from God to the policeman – there is the fear that we will all start stealing. But can it be called morality that out of fear of these authorities we don't steal? Is it religiousness? Isn't their very presence a proof that we are not moral? It is out of the fear of hell and heaven that you don't steal and you don't cheat. Is this a proof of your being moral? No, the only proof of being moral is that you are still moral even when there is nobody to fear. Even when there is nothing to fear, goodness descends on your life; even when there is no reward of any sort, truth and love flow through your life. Freedom is the only criterion of whether a person is moral or immoral. Freedom alone, in all its aspects, will indicate where we stand.

Let me also tell you this: in a way, the fear that the so-called religious people all over the world have – if there is more freedom, immorality will increase – is right because for thousands of years they have imposed a false morality on man. In my view, a true immorality is better than a fake morality. Rather than unnecessarily considering myself to be a gentleman, it is better to remain a wicked man; at least that will be closer to the truth. My understanding that I am a thief will at least be closer to the truth. Once I have a clear awareness of the fact that I am a thief, the possibility of transformation – dropping stealing – is created.

If we become absolutely aware that man is not moral but immoral, that our civilization is fake and our culture all nonsense, if this becomes utterly clear to us, we can do some rethinking about man, about ourselves, about everyone. Then we can think about changing our life in some way, giving it a new direction. But for those who are under the delusion that they are moral and ethical, although deep down they are immoral and unethical, the door to their transformation remains closed.

Once we start thinking independently, the first thing that will happen is that we will be able to see some truths about ourselves. Very few of us are able to see them; we all think we are something which we are not. Someone may be wearing a particular kind of robe and thinks he is a saint. Someone applies sandalwood paste to his forehead, wears a *mala*, wears a sacred thread around his neck and thinks he is religious. Someone may be going to the temple every morning and he thinks that he is earning virtue by this. If we start thinking independently, we will be able to see that there is nothing religious about all these things.

Can someone become a saint by wearing a particular kind of clothes? Or can someone become a saint by eating a particular kind of food? Neither does one becomes a saint by eating a certain food, nor does one become a monk by wearing certain clothes. Food and clothes are utterly trivial things, but saintliness is something unique and precious. No one becomes a saint by doing such trivial things.

We don't ever come to know these truths about ourselves, we don't ever come to know these facts because our thinking is not independent. When everyone says that the people who wear such clothes are saints, we also start saying it. And just because we considered the people wearing such clothes to be saints, one day we put on those clothes and start thinking that we are also saints. It doesn't occur to us to think about what all this has to do with saintliness; we just accept it blindly.

The truth is that it is hard to find a bigger idiot than someone who sees saintliness in the fact that someone is wearing a particular kind of clothes. And a person who sees saintliness in the fact that someone is eating a different kind of food you can only laugh at – nothing else. We never see such ridiculous things because in order to see them we need independent thinking. Only independent thinking will reveal the obvious truth to us. If there is hell within us, it will reveal that hell. We may have covered it with fragrant flowers – that makes no difference. If there is an animal within us, that animal will be revealed in all its nakedness. Unless we see our truth and our reality in detail, no growth is possible in our life.

What am I? It is essential to know this in its utter nakedness. It is necessary for me to know who I am and what I am. Only then can any transformation happen. And what is more surprising is that once you come to know your nakedness in its totality, you simply cannot avoid being transformed. Once you can see the fact that you are a thief, it is impossible for you not to transform. But you don't see it because you donate to charity, do social work. Your stealing is hidden under the cover of charity. That is why all thieves donate. No thief can avoid this, because by doing so he hides the fact of being a thief. He can relax, but then he won't see his nakedness. We simply find many ways to hide all that is worthless in us, all that is evil, wherever we are going wrong.

An irreligious person makes it a point to go to the temple. This is a convenient way of covering himself with spirituality; then self-delusion is easy. "Me, irreligious? Who, me? I am surely not irreligious. Those who don't go to the temple are irreligious but I am certainly religious." This way he hides his inner irreligiousness.

All our morality and all our ethics are only hiding the deep immorality within us – nothing more. That is why there are so many temples and so many people visiting the temples. But where is the religiousness? That is why there are so many religions and so many monks. All over the world there are millions of monks, but the world is in a profound state of misbehavior. When so many bright lights are shining all over the world…

Only yesterday someone was telling me that in the whole world there are one million, two hundred thousand Catholic monks. A friend has come and was telling me about Thailand: out of a population of just forty million, two million are monks. In India, there are five million sannyasins. So in a world where there are so many monks and sannyasins, in a world where there are so many saintly people, there should be light, everywhere light. But they must be extinguished lights, good for the sake of numbers, but they don't radiate any light whatsoever. They are only good at creating noise and trouble, they are only good at creating fights among people – no love arises in them. We are in the grip of hollow morality.

Once your mind becomes capable of thinking, you will see where you really stand. Then the image you will have of yourself may not be very pleasant. Then it will be painful for you to look at it. When the delusion you had about yourself for so long shatters, you may become frightened, but you will have to go through this pain.

Anyone who wants to be reborn will have to go through labor pains. He will have to remove all his clothes, he will have to put all his hollow morality aside, look within himself and ask: "What is within me? Who is there?" If he sees an animal inside, there will be no point in immediately covering himself again with the cloak of morality because it is only due to wearing those clothes that the animal is alive and surviving. So make sure you remove those clothes.

If you are willing to know and see yourself as you really are, that may give you so much pain that you will be ready to change; no other way remains. If a thief can see clearly that he is a thief, if a violent person can see clearly that he is a violent person, it is simply impossible for him to live with stealing or violence any longer, just as no one can live with sickness for a long time. Once he has realized that he is sick, his concern is to treat himself.

These sicknesses are even deeper, these sicknesses touch you deeper than the body. If you become aware of this, you will see that they touch your mind and your being. But man does not become aware of this because he has found so many tricks to divert his mind. He forgets his inner issue; it stays inside him.

Hence whenever the question of putting aside all faiths and beliefs arises, of being ready to see the truth inside us, we feel afraid that immorality will spread, misbehaving will spread. But only when there is misbehavior can it manifest. If it is not there, how can it manifest?

Only those who are ready to see the animal inside them – and not to hide it – are capable of becoming independent. Those who show this much courage, those who show willingness to see their inner animal, have taken the first step. Then they will also have the courage to try and find ways to be free of this animal.

We can only be free of this animal – immorality and misbehavior – when we are alerted to it. But how will those who are asleep be able to free themselves of it? It would be better to have truly dishonest people in the world rather than fake honest people. In that world, it would be possible for something to happen, some transformation would be possible. In a world where there are thieves, it should be clear that they are thieves. At least then they would not be doing charitable works or building temples. In such a world, something can happen.

Society's trap is that we have found false ways to hide our true selves, calling them morality, good conduct – but they are neither. Someone observes a fast at night and he thinks he has become nonviolent. This is the height of idiocy! Is becoming nonviolent so cheap? – if you don't have dinner or drink water you become nonviolent! Nonviolence is such a great revolution that until your soul becomes totally awake, it is simply impossible to achieve it. But you find cheaper ways, the matter is solved, and you become nonviolent. And when one has the comfort of becoming nonviolent so cheaply, then who would be ready to become truly nonviolent? Who would want to go through that revolution and pain? Hence we feel afraid that if someone starts thinking independently, he may start nighttime eating. Then misbehavior will prevail – as if misbehaving will come to an end in the world if everyone stops eating at night. It is not so cheap.

Misbehavior is deeply embedded; it does not depend on what and when you eat. It has pierced deep into your being.

Hence we feel afraid that if we drop all those things imposed on us from outside, if a person becomes independent, who knows when he will start eating and drinking, who knows what kind of clothes he will start wearing, who knows what kind of songs he will start singing on the road. He may even stop going to the temple, stop singing devotional songs. This fear that pervades us, which we all carry, is an indication that the morality we have created in thousands of years is fake and pseudo.

Any moral thinking that is not willing to give man freedom is false. Freedom is the touchstone. If a man is independent as well as moral, the morality is real. My understanding is that this will certainly happen, is bound to happen. If you become independent, something which is beneficial will emerge and become clear to you. In order to have the right diagnosis and right treatment for your disease, it is necessary to have clarity about the disease. Your wounds and boils should be visible, they should not remain hidden; only then can they be treated. Once visible, it will be difficult to leave them untreated.

Those who have attained genuine good conduct are people who have seen their misbehavior. All the people who could rise to godliness are those who have gone deep within themselves and identified their animal. Anyone who wants to touch the sky has to find his roots down in hell, otherwise it is not possible. Anyone who wants to rise up must go deep within himself and expose his inner animal, have a good look at it. Before you can see the godliness you will have to see the animal within you. That is your truth. It is present within you; you cannot run away from it.

Don't be afraid of freedom, be afraid of the false. Be afraid of deception and self-deception. Be afraid of the deceptions that we go on living under. Be afraid of the clothes which we have imposed on ourselves to hide our true face. By disguising yourself as Rama, you will definitely not become Rama. You will be the same person as you are within; deep down you will be the same.

So my understanding is: if you decide to be independent, pain will arise in you, but allow the pain. If some idea, some longing to change has truly arisen in you, look clearly at what is within. Become thoroughly acquainted with your reality. As long as you are dependent in your thinking, you won't be able to change yourself; it is not possible.

Some fourteen or fifteen hundred years ago, a monk went from India to China. An emperor, whose name was Wu, lived there. He had built many temples; he had built many statues and had many scriptures printed.

When he heard about this unique monk coming from India, he went to the border of the state to receive and welcome him. Wu was utterly happy. Because he had built so many temples and statues, printed so many scriptures, all the monks used to tell him: "You are a very religious man, you are a very virtuous man and heaven will be yours."

He used to distribute free food to many monks, so it is obvious that those monks used to sing songs in his praise: "Be relaxed, you will go to heaven. You have given such exceptional donations; you have done such spiritual work. Heaven will be yours."

So when the news of the imminent arrival of this monk – his name was Bodhidharma – spread through the whole of China, Wu went to welcome him. His only concern was what his reward would be for having built so many temples, for having donated billions of rupees. After Bodhidharma had rested, Wu took him aside and asked him, "I have built so many temples and have done so much spiritual work, what will I gain from it?"

Bodhidharma said, "Nothing at all. And since you are expecting something in return, and since you are feeling egoistic about having done so much, you will surely lose something. You won't gain anything whatsoever."

Wu became very nervous. He said, "But all those other monks have been telling me that I will surely go to heaven."

"They praised you because you fed them," said Bodhidharma. "I am telling you the truth: you won't get anything at all, because religion has nothing at all to do with what you have built and created. It has nothing to do with how many statues you have put up. It has nothing to do with how many temples you have built. It only has to do with how much your soul has been transformed."

By building a temple, will your soul be transformed? By putting up statues, will your soul be transformed? For sure no transformation can happen through all this. Your soul remains the same. The man who wanted to have a bigger kingdom in the world, now, in old age, is preparing to conquer the kingdom of heaven as well. That's why he builds temples.

When you wanted a kingdom in this world, you fed the soldiers for free. Now that you want a kingdom in the other world, you feed the monks for free. Where's the difference? When you wanted to have a great kingdom in this world, you extended the boundaries of your empire. Now you want to have a kingdom in the other world, in heaven, so you do charity work and show compassion. But it is all phony, it does not arise out of your being. Behind it is the desire to find something in the other world, so you are acting the same as you did in your desire to find something in this world.

Those who are deeply greedy are not content with just finding a kingdom on earth; they want to have a kingdom in heaven as well. So this so-called religiousness – heaven will be your reward for virtue; if you commit sin, lie and cheat, you will be punished in hell – is based on greed. A morality which is based on greed and the fear of punishment is false. Fear is not the first principle of religiousness. The first principle of religiousness is fearlessness. Wherever there is fear, religiousness cannot exist. Religiousness can only be present where there is fearlessness. And who can be fearless? – only those who are independent. Wherever there is freedom, there will be fearlessness. Where there is no freedom, there will be fear. It is only because of fear that we are dependent.

The question has also arisen out of the fear that immorality may spread, that misbehaving may spread. Immorality and misbehavior are already here, so there is no question of them happening or not. If there is a hell anywhere, it cannot be worse than this earth. What can be worse than this? Twenty-four hours a day we are engaged in violence. Around the clock we are engaged in dishonesty. The whole day we are deceiving ourselves and every-one else.

Those who are very clever are even deceiving God. They pray to God, they sing songs in his praise; they are even influencing God and flattering him. Whatever ways of flattering they are using in the world, they are following the same in praising God. They pray: "You are great, you are the purifier of sins and we are the sinners." They are flattering God, they are bribing him.

Everywhere in the world there is deception – in the temple, in spirituality. Everywhere there is dishonesty. And in such a world of dishonesty and deception we are worried lest there be more immorality! What more immorality can there be? There is absolutely no love in our hearts. There is only hatred and violence. That is why every now and then a war happens, every now and then, somewhere or other, man is fighting.

Someone informed me that in the three thousand years of mankind's history there have been four and half thousand wars. What kind of world is this? Every day a war is happening. And when no war is happening, the preparation for war is going on. Up until now there has been no known period of peace in the history of mankind. We have only known two kinds of periods: a period of war and a period of preparation for war. To date, no human society has known a period of peace. Either people are fighting a war or they are preparing for war. As long as they are making preparations for war, they say a cold war is going on. When they start fighting, a hot war begins, but in both these periods the fight continues. Around the clock fighting continues and every single person is fighting with someone else.

Wherever there is ambition, there will be fighting. Here, you may be sitting relaxed, but every person has his hands in another's pocket. Here, you may be sitting relaxed, but everyone has his hands around another person's neck. Around the clock this goes on. We call this a very moral world, think that this is a moral world – and that if man becomes independent, there will be misbehavior. This is the outcome of man's dependence. If we want to destroy it, we need to gather courage and be concerned about making man independent.

If man becomes independent, if he becomes fearless, if he knows and recognizes the realities of his life, for sure the desire to change all that is bad in him will start arising. The very recognition of the bad becomes the reason for the transformation. Therefore, I don't see any reason why with freedom anything bad can happen.

All this talk about man becoming immoral if he has no faith is just to keep him dependent, to enslave him. People talk about the common people so that man's dependency continues, so that man does not get spoiled, doesn't change. No master is ever ready to release his slaves. He tells people that if they leave him, they will be in difficulty: it is because of him that they have a good life. If they leave him, they will have to face great problems. All masters say the same thing; in fact, that alone is the definition of a master.

Exploiters also talk in the same language just to keep the exploited dependent. The priests and the politicians all over the world unanimously agree on this one point: there is no need for man to become independent. The more dependent a person is, the better; it would be ideal if a person stops thinking altogether. They have thought about how to stop man thinking. They have found ways to brainwash people. If someone is thoughtful, they have thought of ways to brainwash him and make his mind blank. They have invented drugs like mescaline and LSD. If a person starts taking these drugs he will stop thinking on his own.

There are exploiters all over the world; the heads of state or the religious leaders are only the greatest exploiters. No exploiter wants any thought of becoming independent to occur to man, because an independent and thoughtful person will be the cause of a revolution all over the world. Then this rotten and stinking society will not survive. Then this stinking and rotten world will not be tolerated. Thinking will create a great revolution in the world. It will create a great fire and much will be destroyed. So there is an immense fear of man starting to think.

That is why in totalitarian countries – countries where dictatorship exists – people have been prohibited from thinking. If you think, it means death. If you think, you will be shot. All over the world they will try to prevent you from thinking, if not today then tomorrow. Eat, drink, stay home, listen to the radio, read the newspaper – but don't think. Thinking is a very dangerous thing, thinking is a very rebellious thing. Wherever there is thinking there is revolt.

That is why hundreds of ways have been found to stop you from ever thinking on your own; you should simply accept whatever you are told. A politician says that you should just listen to whatever he says. A priest also says the same thing: accept whatever I say. All over the world all those who are in power say the same thing: believe in whatever we say because if you think, there is danger. But there is no danger for you! The danger is to their power, the danger is to their business of exploitation. Hence they make all kinds of arrangements, try to find a thousand and one arguments, to prevent you from thinking.

But remember: nothing is more valuable than freedom. Whatever is said against freedom is dangerous, and it cannot be in the interest of humanity. Freedom is simply a door to reach godliness. Only an independent soul can find that which is beautiful in life, that which is significant. Never a dependent soul.

Other, similar, questions have been raised.

Someone has asked:

> Osho,
> A person is born into a certain society. This society
> educates him, takes care of his upbringing, helps
> him to grow up. So how can someone become free
> of society?

What you say seems to be right. You are born into the society, but that which is born, is not born out of the society. That which is inside you has not come through the society.

When Buddha came back home to his village, the whole village went to welcome him. As his son was coming home after twelve years, his father also went. The whole village had gone to welcome Buddha, but his father had gone to express his anger. His father was under the delusion that Buddha was his son, was born through him, but ran away without informing him.

When he reached there, the first thing he said to Buddha was, "My doors are still open. If you are ready to apologize and come back home, I can forgive you right now. And my heart bleeds seeing you begging. In our community, in our family, no one has ever begged for alms. Seeing a begging bowl in your hands, my whole being writhes in pain. You are a prince, and you don't have to beg for alms. It has never happened in our family."

Do you know what Buddha said? Buddha said, "You are mistaken. I have certainly come through you, but I don't belong to your family. You were like a crossroad I passed through. But my journey has been on a different track for a long time now. Though I was born through you I don't belong to you. No one has ever begged for alms in *your* family as far as I know, but in *my* family one person has always begged for alms. As far as I remember, I have always begged for alms. Yes, I was born through you but I certainly don't belong to you."

Though you have been born into the society, what is inside you does not belong to the society. The society has given you education, given you food, but not a soul. And if you consider this food and education and clothes alone to be the soul, you will be destroyed. Soul is something different and separate. In order to find it, you must go beyond all society's chains.

I am not telling you that if there is a sign on the road asking you to walk on the left, you should walk on the right. No, I am not telling you to start walking on the right or in the middle of the road. This is not freedom, this is simply foolishness. I am not telling you to break those rules. Everyone walks on two feet, but to be independent, you should start walking on all fours – hands and feet – making this a declaration of your freedom. No, I am not saying this.

I am not talking on this level. I am not talking on the level of the body, on the level of social formalities. I am talking on the level of thinking, which is a very deep level within you. *There* you have to become free. Start watching there, awaken your inner eye, and start thinking. There, thinking should be born in you, and there you should become aware of whether what you think and do is right: "Is this fair?" There, you can escape society.

If you are a Hindu, and tomorrow someone comes and tells you to set a mosque on fire because it is a religious act, that is the time to start thinking: how can setting a mosque on fire be a religious act? Or you are a Mohammedan, and tomorrow someone comes and tells you to destroy the statues in a Hindu temple because it is a religious act, now is the time to start thinking: "Is it right? Is it fair?" Can destroying statues be a religious act? This is not about walking on the other side of the road! If any religion tells you to fight and to treat others as your enemies, the time has come when you must think: can religion teach hatred and violence? And it is time for you to free yourself of society.

If the young people of the world can become free of the society in this sense, there will no longer be a reason for war to happen, nor will there be any reason for violence to happen. Then you can neither ask an Indian to fight a Pakistani, nor can you make a Hindu fight a Mohammedan – all these things will look utterly idiotic, foolish, and you will realize what kind of idiotic things man has been doing for thousands of years. You have to become independent on this level.

Someone tells you, "This holy book is the truth, believe in it and worship it and don't ever think anything other than this." Now is the time when you must think: can any book give truth to man? Can you find truth in the words and pages of a book? If you could, everyone in the world would have found truth a long time ago because there are so many holy books and so many religious scriptures. But the more people are burdened with scriptures, the more meaningless for their lives they appear to be.

So you need to think about whether truth can be found through a holy book or whether you yourself will have to search for it. If someone comes and gives you a book, telling you to read it carefully because you will find love through what is written there, wouldn't you doubt that love can be found through a book? You can only find love when it arises in your heart. In the same way you can only find truth when it arises in your heart.

You need to think on all these levels. If someone places a stone statue in front of you and tells you that it is God and you should worship it, you must think. Someone may be worshipping a tree, someone may be worshipping a stone statue in a temple, and someone may be worshipping a book, so it is essential that you think: Are they really God? Wouldn't this kind of worship simply be an ignorant act? Shouldn't I rather search and find out for myself where the source of life is, where the life source of the whole world is? Where is it hiding? Should I search or should I sit holding this stone statue? This is where you need to become independent in thinking, in contemplation.

I am not telling you to be independent of society as far as eating and drinking, wearing clothes, or walking along the street are concerned. These are merely social constraints. This is definitely not the area of the soul. But at the level of the mind, at the level of thinking, your vision has to be alert. It should be thoughtful, it should be thinking on its own and taking its own decisions. Wherever it sees a blind thing happening, it should know to stop, to halt, and to disagree with it. But wherever you see anything meaningful and significant which can take life to a higher plane, you should recognize it and accept it. And if there is anything which unnecessarily takes you into hatred, violence, ignorance, and darkness, you should know to disagree with it. I am asking you to have the intelligence for such independent thinking.

So I am not telling you to drop your clothes or change your food habits or walk zigzag on the street. This is on the level of the society. The question is not at that level. At that level there is no enslavement. On the contrary, it is only because you walk on the left side of the road, and not on the right or in the middle, that you are able to walk along a road at all. I am not telling you to change society's rules about the day-to-day functioning of life.

But as far as the search for truth, the search for life is concerned, as far as the question of reaching the soul is concerned, there you will have to think. There, you will have to contemplate, and there you will have to become independent. Only if you become independent can you find that which is not born out of the society – it was there long before the society existed – and which is not born through your parents. The soul cannot be known through the education you received from parents or the society. In order to know the soul, you must search for and find a totally independent energy.

I hope you have understood my point. Many questions have arisen and I will discuss them tomorrow or the day after tomorrow.

Now for a while we will sit in meditation. A few things to be understood… Meditation is a quest to find complete freedom from the mind. We are so occupied with outward things that we neither look at what is inside us nor do we pay any attention to it. Not only are we occupied with outward things, we are also too occupied and besieged by their influence on our mind. Even if you are alone somewhere, you will still think of what the crowd has given you. You will think of your friends, your enemies, of your business or any other thing – but thinking and contemplation will continue, you won't be able to be alone.

When all thought and contemplation disappear inside you, when all anxiety in the mind calms down and your mind becomes silent, when your silence becomes so intense that no wave arises in your mind... When such silence descends, not even a single wave of thought is there, this state is called meditation.

But you will say, "It is so difficult, it is so arduous," because your mind does not remain quiet, it does not remain silent even for a split second. Some activity or other continues. Some thought or other, some issue or other, some memory or other – either of the past or the present – is continuously going on. Around the clock, the activity goes on. The body does take a rest at times, but there is no real rest. When you sleep at night the dreams go on and during the day, when you are awake, who knows what worries and thoughts are there?

Then how will meditation be possible? Many of you may have sat counting the beads on a *mala* – and it has not happened. Many of you may have sat down reciting the name of God – and it has not happened. And many of you may have prayed and chanted mantras – and it has not happened. So you must have started thinking that it is an utterly difficult thing. But it is not difficult. It is just that whatever you have been doing is wrong; that is why it does not happen.

By counting the beads on a *mala* your mind will not become silent because this has nothing to do with silence. If you chant "Rama, Rama," your mind will also not become silent because chanting is also a kind of disturbance, a trouble in itself. If you go on repeating "Dog, dog" or "Cat, cat," people will call you mad, but if you go on saying "Rama, Rama," people will say you are very religious.

It is one and the same thing – there is no difference. Repeating a word again and again is simply a sign of unconsciousness; your mind won't become silent. Yes, it is possible that if you are stubborn and you continue doing it, your mind may go to sleep. But there is a great difference between sleeping and becoming silent.

When a mother wants to put her baby to sleep, she starts humming a lullaby, "Go to sleep my baby, go to sleep my baby," or uttering some other nonsense. Perhaps she thinks that the song is very melodious; that is why the child goes to sleep. But it is the outcome of boredom, and certainly not the outcome of any melodious song. The child simply gets bored. Listening to the same lullaby again and again, after a while he goes to sleep. Similarly if you go on chanting "Rama, Rama," your mind may get bored and tired and go to sleep.

Don't think that sleepiness is silence. You can get that from opium, from alcohol as well. There is no difference between the two. Smoking opium, drinking alcohol, or taking sleeping pills – there are a thousand and one tranquilizers available to put you to sleep. And there are also very old and popular medicines of the same kind.

If you go on repeating any word again and again, your mind will get bored and tired. Yes, if you get up before the boredom sets in, that is a different thing. But if you continue, your mind will go to sleep. When you wake up after that sleep you will feel great peace. But it was just sleep, created by repeating the same words again and again. It was not silence; there was nothing special about it. I don't call such things meditation. None of them are.

So what do I call meditation? Meditation is when one is in total awareness, not when one is asleep, not when one falls asleep.

The meditation that we are going to do now is an experiment in awareness. You have to sit, being totally aware of whatever is happening around you. A leaf may shake, a bird may chirp, a dog may bark, a child may cry, someone may cough, other things may be happening. There will also be many other noises around. As your mind becomes silent, you will start hearing softer sounds as well. You will start hearing the chirping of a small bird which up to now you could not hear.

All around you there is a world of happenings, and you have to sit being totally aware of them.

CHAPTER 4

answers come through consciousness

My beloved ones.

Yesterday we contemplated a little on the thought-less state. Ordinarily man lives in thought-less states. One is the bondage of desire and the other is of faith and belief. At the level of the body, man is dependent, and also at the level of the mind. At the level of the body it is not possible to be independent, but at the level of the mind it is possible. Yesterday I spoke to you on a few things about this. Today I will talk about how man can become independent at the level of the mind, how the thinking state can be born in him.

If thinking is not born, man can neither have any experience in life nor can there be any creativity. Then we will simply live in vain and die in vain. Our life will be a futile effort because where there is no thinking there is no vision; where there is no thinking, man simply does not have any energy to see or walk on his own. For a person who does not see on his own, does not walk on his own, does not live on his own, it will be just impossible to have any experience that can liberate him, to have any experience that can fill his heart with love and illuminate his being. For anything to happen in life, you must first have eyes.

What I mean by the thinking state is that you should have eyes, what I mean is the ability to think on your own. But I don't mean a crowd of thoughts. We all have a crowd of thoughts within us, but we don't have *thinking* within us. So many thoughts go on moving within us, but the power of thinking has not been awakened.

It is really surprising: the more someone has thoughts moving within him, the less he has the ability to think. If someone is filled with scattered thoughts, a constant movement of thoughts and a crowd of thoughts, his ability to think lies dormant. Only a man who can drop the crowd of thoughts can attain the power of thinking. Hence, if you are constantly occupied with thoughts, it does not mean that you are capable of thinking. The reason why so many thoughts go on moving inside you is because you are *incapable* of thinking.

If a blind man wants to leave a building, a thousand and one thoughts occur to him: how should he leave? Which door should he go through? How should he get up? Whom should he ask? But if someone who has eyes wants to leave, he simply gets up and walks out. Inside him there is no movement of thoughts as to how he should do it. He can see the door, so he simply gets up and goes outside.

The ability to think is the ability to see. Once thinking happens in your life, you start seeing. But having a crowd of thoughts does not give you the ability to see. On the contrary, your ability to see gets hidden amidst the crowd of thoughts; it is concealed. So first let me tell you this, and then we will think about how you can awaken the power of thinking.

But before I speak about it, first I must tell you that all thoughts moving in the crowd of thoughts are aliens; they are not your own. Hence when I say that thinking should be born in you, I am not saying that you should read the scriptures and books and accumulate many thoughts. By that thinking will not be born in you. To be a scholar is not to attain thinking. To accumulate a lot of knowledge, knowing many doctrines, many answers, and much of philosophy is not thinking.

So what does it mean to think? Thinking means the awakening of your consciousness concerning the problems of life, the emergence of solutions to life's problems out of your consciousness. When life confronts you with questions, you should not have borrowed answers; your own answers should manifest.

Every day, life creates problems, but our answers are borrowed, so none of the problems in our life ever get solved. The problems are ours but the solutions are given by others, so they are never in tune with each other. Every day, life creates questions; every day, life creates problems, but we only have ready-made answers, answers we have been given. We live our lives according to those answers. The solutions fail and so the problems are victorious.

Let me tell you a short story. Perhaps then you may understand how old and stale our solutions are, and why we are defeated.

In a village there were two rival temples. All temples are against each other. If there are different gambling places and pubs in the village there may be no rivalry between them, but if there are temples there is rivalry. It should not be so, but temples have always been against each other. The day there is no rivalry between temples it will be possible to build a temple of God. But as long as there is a rivalry it will not be possible. Until that day it will be called God's temple, inside the statues will be of God, but the Devil will be hidden inside it. Rivalry is a weapon of the Devil.

So in that village there was rivalry between the two temples. Their rivalry was so strong that the priests would not even look each other in the eye. They were so much against each other that the devotees of one temple would not even go to the other temple. In their scriptures it was written that it is better to die getting crushed under a mad elephant's feet than to take shelter in the rival's temple. Visiting the rival's temple was considered to be worse than dying under a mad elephant's feet!

The priests of the temples each had a small boy who used to take care of them and do work like bringing vegetables from the market. Since they were small boys, they were not yet in the grip of the disease the old people were suffering from. So sometimes when they met in the street, they would talk to each other.

Older people want to infect small children with their diseases as early as possible. If they don't, they feel afraid that the children will go astray.

Hence the priests of both temples used to constantly warn their boys: "Beware, never go near the other temple. Never talk to anyone from the other temple." But children are after all children; they had not yet grown up and were still innocent. So occasionally they used to meet each other.

One day both boys were going to the market when they met on the way. The temples had names: one was called the Temple of the South and the other was the Temple of the North. The boy from the Temple of the North asked the other boy, "Where are you going?"

The boy from the Temple of the South answered, "Wherever my feet take me."

The boy from the northern temple was quite confused. Now how can the conversation go any further? When the other boy said that he was going wherever his feet were taking him, the conversation got stuck.

He came back and told the priest of his temple, "Today I was defeated by the boy from the other temple. I asked him where he was going and he said wherever his feet were taking him. Then I just couldn't think of anything else to say."

The priest said, "This is really bad. To be defeated by the servant of that temple is humiliating. Tomorrow you go prepared. Ask him the same question again and if he gives the same answer ask him, 'What if you had no feet, would you go somewhere or not?' Then he will be trapped. Then he won't know what to say."

The next day they met again. The boy from the northern temple asked the other boy, "Where are you going?"

But today the answer changed. The boy said, "Wherever the winds take me."

Now the first boy was in a difficulty. Although he had a ready-made answer, how he could he give it? So he went back to his temple again and told the priest, "I was in great difficulty. That boy is really dishonest. He simply changed his answer."

The priest said, "This is really bad. Tomorrow ask him the same question again and if he says, 'Wherever winds take me,' ask him, 'What if there were no winds, where would you go in life?'"

He again went to the market and again the boys met on the way. He asked the other boy, "Where are you going?" But that boy changed his answer once again and said, "I am going to the market to fetch vegetables."

The boy went back to the temple and told the priest, "This is so difficult. That boy simply keeps changing his answers. Today he said he was going to the market to fetch vegetables. Again I came back defeated."

Life also changes every day. Yesterday's answers are of no help today and all of us only have yesterday's answers. We have answers which we have learned from others, the answers we have been taught, the answers from scriptures, doctrines, and the unconsciousness of thousands of years. Every day we confront life with the same answers, but life changes every day. Then we blame life, saying that it is dishonest and inconsistent, but we don't blame our unconsciousness for our unconsciousness.

The suffering is not caused by the inconsistency of life. The suffering is in our unconsciousness: that is why we are never in tune with life. Wherever there is life, there is liveliness; wherever there is life, there is momentum; wherever there is life, there is transformation and change. There is a revolution every moment, and every moment everything is new.

Where there is death, there is unconsciousness; where there is death, there is no change; where there is death, there is no revolution of any sort. Everything is at a standstill, on hold, closed. Life is open, life is liberated. Don't be angry at the inconsistency of it, rather look at your unconsciousness. Don't be concerned about life's ever-changing forms; be concerned about your unchanging mind.

It's not surprising that when our mind clings to solutions and scriptures, it is incapable of experiencing and knowing life. Life goes on flowing, but the mind is unable to keep pace with it; it always lags behind. We are always a step behind, so life starts becoming a suffering and a burden, it starts turning into failure. The thinking state means that your mind should be moving at the same pace as life.

But you must have heard that the movement of the mind is not a good thing. You must have heard that the inconsistency of the mind is a very bad thing. You must have read and heard that this inconsistency is the whole trouble. You must have heard people saying that you should halt the inconsistency of the mind, bring the mind to a standstill, kill the movement of the mind – the quicker the mind comes to a halt the better.

I want to tell you that the inconsistency of the mind is a significant thing. Its inconsistency should be so intense, the movement should be so intense, that it is able to keep pace with the movement of life. It should not remain behind life. The more the mind moves, the more powerful it will be. So you are not to make mind dull. You are not to make it lifeless by counting *mala* beads and chanting, "Rama, Rama." You are not to bring it to a halt. A halted mind simply cannot be creative.

Those societies which wanted and tried to make the mind dull were unfortunate. They could neither give birth to science nor could they invent or create anything. For thousands of years those societies have lived under the burden of not being able to create or invent. How could they? It cannot be. If we kill the movement of the mind, we will attain a kind of unconsciousness. But life is not meant for being unconscious, dull; it is meant for being utterly conscious. Your mind should have movement, your mind should not stop at dead solutions. On the contrary, it should be able to keep pace with the problems of life.

Thinking means a moving mind. Thinking means: if there is a problem you should not try to find the answer in your memory, as that answer will be old and stale. If I ask you "Does God exist?" and you try to look for the answer in your memory – "Yes, I read in the Gita that there is a God"; or "I read it in the Koran"; or "I heard from someone"; or "My father, my grandfather, used to say that God exists" – this answer will come from the memory. Hence it will be dead, it will be stale, and it will be borrowed from others.

When life creates a question, put memory aside and don't allow your memory to speak. Tell your memory to excuse you. And once your memory becomes totally silent, your consciousness will have to find its own answer.

It is possible that it may not find any answer. It is possible that no answer may arise out of it, but that too will be very significant. If the question remains, and no answer arises from your consciousness, only then will your consciousness become awake. It will become awake in order to find the answer. In the quest for an answer, the layers of the consciousness will open and consciousness will awaken. Don't worry if no answer comes. If you immediately accept the answer from your memory, there is no reason for the consciousness to awaken, there is no way. What your consciousness is supposed to do is being done by the memory; there is no need for the consciousness to wake up.

Thinking is born when you leave it to the consciousness to

do its work and don't accept any answer from the memory. Every time there is a problem, we ask the memory to give us an answer; we simply extract our answers from our memory. Our educational system, the religious scriptures and the priests, also teach us the same thing: let the memory do the work. They all teach you to accept ready-made answers. But it is suicidal for you; it is suicidal for anyone. The answers from the memory are mechanical. As they have not come out of your consciousness, they neither help your consciousness to grow nor help it to evolve. On the contrary, they kill it, they make it dull. You must surely have heard that nowadays there are computers which can be fed with all kinds of answers. Very soon man will not need to remember anything. Everything can be fed into the computers and then answers can be extracted from them.

Your memory is also a machine. Perhaps you will be surprised to know that very soon it will be possible to transfer one person's memory to another person. There have already been successful experiments in this area. Someone's complete memory can be transferred to someone else because memory is simply a machine. Memory is simply an inner chemical change. If one could remove all those tissues from the part of the brain where memory is stored, and put them into another person's brain, then, without that person having studied it, all that knowledge will be available to him. Recently scientists have succeeded in their primary experiments with this. One person's experience can be transferred to someone else without that person having to go through that experience. One person's memory, along with all its chemicals, can be transferred to another person's brain.

Memory is utterly mechanical; it is not knowing, not your own experience; it is a storehouse, just as you may store money in a safe. If you take the safe and give it to a poor person, he will become rich. Similarly thoughts are stored in your memory. Up to now it was not possible for us to transfer memory, but now it is possible. Very soon it will become possible to easily transfer a person's whole memory to someone else. Then a scholar's death will not be a problem: the moment he dies we can transfer all his memory to children. Then scholarship will not remain a hollow thing; it will be sold in the market. Even now it is being sold in the market. Even now it is not of much value. You may repeat and memorize certain things, but even now machines can also do the job of repeating.

Memory is a mechanical process in the brain. It does not give birth to knowing, with it no thinking is born. On the contrary, memory doesn't allow thinking to be born. Whenever an opportunity comes for you to think, your memory simply gives the answer – thinking cannot be born. Whenever life asks you a question, your memory gives the answer and your consciousness simply remains silent. It should be the other way round. When life asks you questions, your memory should remain silent and your consciousness should have to find the answers.

So, in order to begin to think, in order to flourish in thinking, you should understand this first key: train your memory to keep quiet, teach your memory to remain silent and tell your memory not to always give the answer to every problem. I am not telling you to leave small things – such as where your house is, what your name is – to your consciousness to give you the answer. I am not saying tell your memory to be silent when you come back from somewhere, to stand in the road and start thinking about where your house is. Memory is certainly useful at a certain level. Memory is useful at the level of matter, at the level of the world, or if you want to study engineering or medicine. But on the level of self-knowing, memory can be fatal.

Memory has a utility. All machines have a utility, memory too. At the ordinary level of the mind, memory is useful. If it were not there, it would become impossible for you to live. But if you put the surface aside, at a much deeper level of life, memory is of no use at all. There, the answers given by the memory prove to be absolute lies. There, the memory – all our learning, whatever we have heard from others – should remain silent. Then we can search for the answer ourselves, go on a quest, enter the unknown and become acquainted with it.

For thinking to take birth, in order to know the unknown truth, the unknown life, the unknown soul, God, it is essential for the memory to stay silent. Whenever you come across the deeper problems of life and your memory starts speaking, tell it to be silent. Memory should not be an obstruction. Say good-bye to it, so that your own consciousness can explore.

The first key for the birth of thinking is teaching your memory to remain silent. Memory constantly goes on talking, and because it is of help in the mundane things of the life, the delusion is created that it will be useful in the deeper search of life as well – but it cannot be of any help there. The moment the concept of silencing your memory becomes clear to you, all the scriptures, all doctrines, will also become silent because they only exist in the memory. Immediately all the *tirthankaras* and all the avatars will become silent. Then all knowledge will become silent; that also only exists in the memory. You will go on a search alone, your consciousness will go on a search alone.

When you are confronted with the question of going on a search, when there is an intense inspiration to explore, and when there is no other option, only in that moment does the search begin. Only through that pressure can the search begin – then your being looks forward to it.

If we allow other people to do our work, slowly, slowly our being becomes dull and sleepy. If all the work is done by others, our being will go to sleep completely. At the level of body it is fine for others to do our work, but at the level of the soul it is fatal.

Confucius has written that he once went to a village – this incident happened over two thousand years ago – and he saw an old man pulling water from a well with a bucket tied to a rope.

Both the old man and his son were yoked to bamboos – whereas usually in those days an ox was yoked to pull water from a well. Confucius thought that perhaps these people were not aware that the work they were doing themselves could be done by horses or oxen.

He went and told the old man, "My friend, are you not aware that nowadays in big cities and towns people have started using horses and oxen to do this kind of work?"

The old man said, "Please speak softly, lest my son hear this. And come back after a while."

Confucius was surprised. Why had the old man said this to him?

After a while he went back and the man said to him, "Now tell me what you wanted to say. I have also heard that nowadays people use horses and oxen for this kind of work, but I am afraid that if my son comes to know about this, he will also start getting his work done by horses and oxen. But that's not the end of the matter. If we let others do the work for us, our own energy diminishes. Today my son has the strength of a horse. But if horses take over his work, tomorrow he will lose all his strength and energy."

Certainly the process won't end there. Soon we will also start employing others to do all kinds of work. Then a time will come when all the work will be done by machines. But then what will man do?

So the old man told Confucius, "You better go away and keep your invention to yourself. Don't bring it to this village."

Later on Confucius told his disciples, "That old man taught me an amazing thing. Most probably, some unfortunate day or other, we *will* get other people to take over our work. Then life will be very difficult."

Camus has written in a novel that he could imagine a time when people will ask their servants to make love on their behalf.

It sounds frightening. Camus said, "Someday or other man will think, "Why should I take the trouble of making love? Why not ask the servants to do it? Or if some machine can be invented I will get it done by machines as well." It looks surprising to us. We just cannot imagine that someday we will ask machines to do the work of lovemaking.

As far as knowing is concerned, we have left it to machines. Memory is simply a machine, and because we have left knowing to it, our own consciousness does not awaken. For our own consciousness to awaken, all the burden and pain and sting of life's problems must touch our consciousness, pierce our consciousness. Then it is disturbed and starts arising, it starts becoming awake. It is only when life hurts us that something awakens in us. Only when life challenges us, does the energy rise up and give the answer.

Don't function through memory. When it comes to the deeper problems of life, when it comes to knowing the truth, godliness, the soul, tell your memory to be silent. Only then will thinking be born.

By thinking you may not necessarily get the answer. There may be many answers for which there are no words, which can only be found in silence. If you ask, it is possible that your consciousness may simply remain quiet. But even in that quietness, even in that silence, a solution will start coming that will transform your being. It is not that you will then be able to answer other people's questions – what will happen is that *you* will have a totally different life. The answer, the solution, will be the transformation of your being.

The answer will not come in the form of words. You may ask and your consciousness remains silent: you may not get any answer from within. Maybe you ask, "Is there a God?" but no answer comes in the form of yes or no. It won't come like this. An answer which comes as "Yes" will simply come out of memory created by the theists, the answer that comes as "No" will come out of memory created by the atheists. Even if you don't use your memory at all – only your consciousness tries to search for an answer – it is possible that none may come. My understanding is that no verbal answer will come.

But in that silence, in that state of no-answer, your being starts finding a solution. Although a solution does not come in the form of words, from the next day onward, your life starts taking a totally different turn. Then if someone asks you, "Is there a God?" you may not be able to say yes or no, but you can show him through your life. "Look at my life, perhaps you may come to know," because in that life there will be godliness.

Perhaps you may tell him, "Look into my eyes, and when looking you may find an answer." Or you may tell him, "Listen to my heartbeat and in that heartbeat you may find an answer." A solution attained in silence will envelop your whole life. Whether God exists or not is not a matter of a verbal or intellectual answer; it is simply a prayer arising out of your whole life. It is not a matter of your words. It is a prayer, a fragrance, music that arises out of your life.

Once a man came to Buddha and asked him some questions. Buddha said to him, "If you really want to find answers to your questions, go somewhere else. I don't give answers, I only give solutions."

The man was puzzled. He asked, "Is there a difference between a solution and an answer?"

Buddha said, "There is a great difference. Answers are intellectual, verbal. But solutions are not intellectual. They are spiritual, of the inner. Answers are in words and solutions come from meditation. I can give you answers, but solutions come from within. So I am certainly able to give you answers, but if you want to find solutions, then you have to wait. Answers can be given immediately, but solutions will take years, even your whole life, even numerous lives. If you have that much patience, wait."

The man said, "I am tired of trying to find answers. I have been searching for the last thirty years, but whoever I meet simply gives me an answer. I get answers but the questions still remain; they do not disappear. So I am ready to wait, I will wait patiently."

Buddha said, "Stay here. After a year, on the same day as today, ask me those questions again."

He stayed. During that year he was initiated into the practice of meditation, taught how to remain silent.

We know how to remain silent on the outside, but it is very difficult to remain silent within; it is not at all easy. One who becomes silent from within comes to know all there is. There is no greater key for knowing truth or godliness than to become silent within. But what we see happening is that those who try to know God simply fill themselves with the Gita, the Koran or the Bible. How can they become silent? Every morning they read the scriptures and memorize the words. And the day they have memorized the Gita completely, they start enjoying the feeling that they are knowledgeable. They have simply filled themselves. But it is only those who really empty themselves from within who come to know.

For a year Buddha taught him the science of emptying himself. "Become utterly empty from within, say good-bye to everything that is within you. The day your inner space becomes empty, that same day a solution will come."

A year passed. After a year Buddha told him, "Now you can ask."

But the man started laughing. He said, "As I became more and more empty from within, my questions disappeared. Those questions had also filled me inside. Now I don't have any question whatsoever."

Buddha said, "Did any answer come?"

He said, "No answer of any sort came, but now I don't need any answer. I have attained the solutions that I had been looking for. My whole life has been transformed."

Attainment is in the transformation of life and not in finding an answer. Thinking will not give you an answer, but it will bring the transformation of your life. So the first key is to say good-bye to the memory, to silence your memory and to tell your memory to wait.

The second key is: live with the question patiently. Those in a hurry to find an answer will become dependent on the memory. If you want a quick answer, the memory will give you the answer instantly, but this precept is all about waiting patiently. If no answer comes, wait. Just ask the question and be silent; don't accept anyone else's answer. Just ask the question and become silent. Try experimenting with this.

Try doing this experiment. Ask yourself "What is love?" and just remain silent. If any answer comes through books and scriptures, just ignore it; don't let it come between you and the question. Ask "What is love?" then be silent, wait. The answer to what love is won't come in words, but slowly, slowly you will find that this question – "What is love?" – has started piercing your being. Slowly, slowly you will find that love has started arriving in your life. Don't give any answer and your life will start filling with love. One day you will find that the question has disappeared and your life has become filled with love.

Ask "Who am I?" but don't give the answer "I am soul"; or "I am this"; or "I am that." Everywhere you are being taught such answers: "You are a pure awakened soul"; "You are infinite knowing"; "You are this or that." No, don't give any such answers. Ask "Who am I?" and become silent. At the time of going to sleep ask yourself "Who am I?" When you become awake, again ask yourself "Who am I?" And don't use any of those answers that you have heard from others. Just be silent and let this question "Who am I?" go on descending in your life. Sleeping, awake, working, whenever you can remember, ask yourself "Who am I?" And be quiet, don't give any answer, don't give any answer from your side. And slowly, slowly this question will drop, and you will attain a solution within. No words will form, but you will know who is in.

A person who gives answers is mistaken. A person who has a question silences the memory – keeps it from giving the answer – then waits patiently without finding an answer. One day, he will find a solution. This is what I mean by thinking. By thinking I mean to ask yourself deep within and wait patiently.

Patience is a wonderful thing. A person sows a seed and then waits patiently for the seed to sprout. The seed will one day sprout, the leaves will come, the flowers will blossom and the tree will bear fruit. It is an immense waiting. If you don't want to wait until the flowers blossom, you can buy plastic flowers that are available in the market. You can find them immediately; you don't have to wait for long to obtain those flowers. Similarly someone who really wants to go in search of life should simply sow the seed of the question and remain silent. He should not be in a hurry to find the answer. If he finds the answer quickly, it will be borrowed, stale, from someone else. It will be of the marketplace, a plastic flower. That answer will not have any life, it won't be alive.

Just sow the seed of the question and don't bother about the answer. Wait silently. Sow the seed of the question and wait for the answer, for the solution. Out of that question a bud will sprout. Out of a seed, which seems to have no life, looks utterly dead, a living bud sprouts. The seed breaks open, rots away but gives rise to a bud. Then out of that bud, life grows and brings forth the flowers.

The answer, which at first you cannot see, is hidden in the question. Let the question go deep into the soil of your heart, don't be in a hurry. Let that question remain within you, let it melt in your heart, let it melt and break open. Then a bud will sprout and an answer will come. But you will have to wait patiently. And the longer one patiently waits, the quicker the seed can sprout. It will bear the fruit and flowers of a solution, and your life will be filled with its fragrance.

It is necessary for us to sow within ourselves all the deeper questions concerning our life. But we don't sow the seeds; we simply want to get rid of the questions. And the only way we know to get rid of them is to start asking answers from others so that we can feel content.

For those who want to think, it is the question that is meaningful not the answer, but for those who want to believe, it is the answer that is meaningful not the question. If you want to believe, store answers, but if you want to think, put the answers aside and collect the questions, the inquiry, the problems. There is a difference between the two.

A person who believes simply collects the answers, but a person who thinks stores the question deep within him, he puts his whole being into the question. A person who thinks is like a farmer. He sows the seed of the question, whereas a person who believes fills his storehouse with answers, not with questions. A person who accumulates answers becomes a scholar but a person who sows the question attains wisdom.

Someone who sows the question then toils and waits, until one day he attains the flowers of wisdom. A person who collects beliefs, answers, ready-made solutions and doctrines, immediately harvests the fruit and becomes a pundit. Ask him any question and he starts giving answers. But in his life neither a ray of knowing bursts nor does any fundamental change happen. If you ask him about truth, he can give the answer – but there is no truth in his life. If you ask him about love, he can write scriptures on it – but there is not a trace of love in his life.

It is possible that someone who sows the seed within himself may find it difficult to say or write anything about love, it may be difficult for him to say anything about truth – but the fragrance of love and truth starts pervading his life.

There was once a Baul mystic in Bengal. A Hindu pundit went to see him. The Baul mystics constantly talk of love. They sing songs of love, their prayers are of love, they live in love, and they walk in love. The Hindu pundit went to see him and asked the Baul mystic, "Does God exist?"

He said, "I don't know, but love exists. And anyone who comes to know love will one day come to know godliness as well."

The Hindu pundit asked him, "What love? Which love? Do you know how many kinds of love there are?"

The Baul mystic was amazed. He said, "I have certainly experienced love, but I don't know about kinds. How can there be different kinds of love?"

The Hindu pundit started laughing – a pundit always laughs at those who know – and said, "Don't you even know this? There *are* different kinds of love. There are five kinds of love. So through which kind of love can you find godliness?"

The Baul mystic simply kept quiet. The pundit took out a book from his bag, opened it, and said, "My scripture describes five kinds of love." And he read out loud the subtle definitions of each kind of love. After reading them out, he asked the Baul mystic, "So how did you find it? How did you feel it? How did you like this analysis of love? Are these different kinds of love? Right or wrong? How did you feel listening to them?"

You will be amazed to know what the mystic said. He started dancing and singing a song. The song had a unique meaning. What he sang was: "You are asking me how I felt. When you started describing different kinds of love, do you know what I felt? I felt as if some goldsmith had come to a garden of flowers carrying the stone on which he tests gold. I felt as if he had repeatedly rubbed the flowers on that stone to check which flower is real and which is fake."

The Baul mystic said to the pundit, "Since I came to know love, all the kinds of love have disappeared. When I came to experience love, all distinctions dropped. When I came to experience love, neither I remained nor the object of my love remained.

When I experienced love, only love remained. There were neither different kinds of love nor was there any distinction, no duality, no lover, and no one who was loved – only love itself. Only those who have not known and experienced love, those who have just read the scriptures, think that there is such a thing as different kinds of love."

In the search for life there are two directions: one is the direction of the scholar and the other is of knowing. Someone who takes the direction of the scholar gets lost forever because he simply does not have anything other than words. Someone who goes in the direction of knowing, slowly, slowly his words go on disappearing. In the end, he has nothing except the experience of the wordless.

A person who accumulates thoughts will become a scholar. A person who gives birth to thinking – gives birth to the ability to think, asks questions and challenges his consciousness and then waits for the answer – in his life, knowing is born. It is not through thoughts that you attain knowing but through thinking. Not by collecting thoughts, but by giving birth to thinking. We all make the mistake of collecting thoughts and imagining we have attained thinking. No, this way we won't attain thinking, we won't attain awareness and we won't attain wisdom.

I have told you two keys for attaining wisdom, for attaining thinking: first, let your memory become silent. Beware of the memory as the memory is dangerous, the memory is utterly deceptive. One who falls in the delusion of memory goes astray. Second, ask questions but don't be in a hurry for the answer. Sow the seeds of the question in your being, allow the question to revolve there, let it echo there. Allow the question to intensify there as long as possible. Let the question move in your mind, let it have momentum and don't be in a hurry to find the answer.

Don't accept any borrowed answer. If answers come, go on rejecting them. A moment should come when there is no answer;

only the question remains. The question should go on piercing your being like an arrow. Wait and watch, watch patiently. One day, out of that question the answer will come.

The same soul that asked the question is capable of giving the answer. But if we start accepting others' answers, there is no reason for the soul to give an answer. The same soul which created the quest, created the problem, is capable of finding the solution. Remember, if there is a problem, there is a solution as well. If there is a question, if there is a quest, there is an answer as well. So let the same center of being from where the quest is arising find the solution. Don't be in a hurry, and don't accept any borrowed solution from anywhere. That borrowed solution becomes an obstacle to the arrival of the real solution.

I have told you these two keys in order to give birth to thinking. If you avoid the thought-less state, avoid beliefs, prevent memory from giving answers, and constantly go on trying to awaken thinking, one day thinking will surely be born in you – and your whole life will be transformed. In that moment of experiencing, you will find that all beliefs, doctrines, truth, and scriptures, have all, in a deeper sense, become clear to you, have become evident.

A person who follows his own thinking one day attains authentic trust, authentic faith, and an experience which leaves no room for doubt. He has attained it by himself, he has known it himself. Only that truth which we have found on our own is unquestionable. A truth which has been found by someone else, no matter who he is, no matter how great a person he is – even if he is God himself – cannot be indubitable for you and me. That is why behind all these so-called beliefs, disbelief is hidden, that is why behind all these beliefs, doubt and suspicion remain. We keep it hidden, but it is present all the same.

You may believe in the existence of God. But if you search a little inside yourself, you will find more than one thought which doubts whether God exists. You may believe there is a soul, but hidden inside you is a seed saying, "Who knows whether the soul exists or not?" The more firmly you believe in the existence of the soul or God, the more there will be doubt as well. Otherwise, against what are you creating that firmness? It is only against that doubt. You are simply creating that firmness against the doubt present inside you. You believe in it very intensely so that you forget about that doubt present inside you. It *is* present inside you; it cannot disappear. It may remain hidden, but it is real. All this firmness and faith are fake. All these beliefs have simply been imposed on you. Only the doubt is real.

Hence I told you yesterday to allow that doubt to surface. Don't fall prey to fake beliefs. If you really want to attain the state of authentic faith and trust someday, let that real doubt become manifest, allow it to ask, allow the questions to arise, and allow the problems it brings. And when the problems come, don't immediately find an answer.

One day the answer will come. If you wait, one day the solution will arrive. It will transform your whole being, your whole life. Only the solution that transforms your whole life is real. And no solution has ever come, can ever come, except through one's own thinking.

Today I have told you a few things about the thinking state. Tomorrow I will talk to you about the state of no-thought. I am explaining to you how through these three steps – the thoughtless state, the thinking state, and the state of no-thought – the truth of life can be found.

I am thankful that you have listened to my talk with such love and silence.

CHAPTER 5

the thinking state:
your center, your being, your soul

This morning I spoke to you about the thinking state.

Someone has asked:

> Osho,
> When any thought, be it from a person or from a
> scripture, gets assimilated, it becomes one's own
> thought...

It is often said that when you assimilate any thought it
becomes your own thought. But what do you mean by assimilation of thought? Can any thought be assimilated? In my view, a
thought cannot be assimilated. Yes, one may have the delusion
that one has assimilated a thought. If we insistently go on believing
in some thought, if we constantly go on thinking some thought,
if we constantly go on repeating it, we can create a kind of self-
delusion that this thought has entered us.

For example…

A few days ago, a wandering monk came to meet me and he said, "I see God everywhere – in trees, in animals, in birds. Where-ever I look I see only God there."

The devotees accompanying him had come first, and in his praise they told me, "The person we are going to introduce to you sees God everywhere. In every single leaf he has a glimpse of God. He sees God and God's image everywhere."

Then the monk came. I asked him, "If you are seeing God everywhere, have you attained this state by repeatedly thinking a thought or have you attained it in a state of no-thought? Have you been repeatedly thinking that God is everywhere? Have you been constantly and persistently remembering that God is every-where, in flowers, in leaves, and in plants?"

He said, "For twenty years I had been practicing it. Around the clock I go on thinking the same sacred thought. Now I have started seeing God everywhere."

I told him, "Just do me a favor. For a week stop thinking this thought, and after a week come and tell me what happened."

He said, "That would be very difficult. If I stop thinking this thought, I will stop seeing God."

For twenty years he has been thinking this thought: God is everywhere. If he stops thinking it for a week God will disap-pear! He has created a kind of delusion in his mind that God is everywhere. It is nothing but an imaginary state of mind, a pro-jection of the mind. It is only because he is constantly thinking a particular thought that this delusion of seeing God everywhere has been created in him. It is simply a dream.

This is how a thought gets assimilated. It is not the experi-ence of a thought from within, but rather man's ability to see inside himself whatever he imagines is there. If a person con-stantly goes on thinking of something…

Just today a friend came and told me, "I constantly go on thinking, 'I am not the body, I am not the mind, I am a soul.' Should I continue with this thought or not?"

I told him, "Never do this, even by mistake. If you go on repeatedly thinking this, you will start feeling 'I am neither body, nor am I mind, I am just a soul,' but this feeling would be fake. It is simply a delusion created by the constant repetition of the thought."

This is not experiencing. This is self-hypnosis, it is auto-hypnosis. If you go on repeating a thought again and again, it is not difficult to have this feeling. And the extent to which self-hypnosis can go is inconceivable.

When I was studying, I had a teacher who was a devotee of Krishna. He constantly used to think that he should be able to see Krishna everywhere. I told him, "As long as you don't see him everywhere you are fortunate. The day you start seeing him everywhere, you will be almost in a state of madness because that will be a projection of your thought. It won't be your experience."

He said, "How is that possible? Unless something really exists, you can't start seeing it just by imagining it to be there. Just by imagining it, how can I start seeing God or Krishna in everyone? Only when Krishna exists, can I see him." I just listened to his views. That day I did not say anything to him.

The university he used to teach at was only a mile's distance from his residence. The next day I went there and met his neighbor's wife. I told her my professor's name and said to her, "Tomorrow morning as soon as he leaves the house, tell him that he looks very sick. Ask him if he is not well or if something is wrong. Whatever he replies, write his exact words on a piece of paper. Don't change a single word."

His office clerk lived a short distance from his place. I told him the same thing. "When the professor passes by, tell him that he looks bit pale. Ask him what the matter is. And write down whatever he says, don't make the slightest change. Whatever he says, just write it down."

I told this to ten or fifteen people who resided on the lane leading to the university. All of them asked, "What is going on?"

I said, "I am just experimenting with something and I need your help."

Next day when the professor left his house, his neighbor's wife said to him, "What is the matter? Today you look very sick."

He said, "Sick? I am absolutely hale and hearty. What sickness? I am not at all sick. I am absolutely fine."

As he walked down that lane toward the university his office clerk said, "Today you look very sick."

The professor replied "Actually, I do feel a bit sick. I haven't been feeling well since last night."

When he went further down the lane he met three or four students. They also said the same: "Today, even from behind we can see that your legs seem to be shaking. Are you not well?"

He said, "Since last night I have been feeling a bit unwell. I did not feel like coming to the university today but I thought..."

He entered the university and met two or three girls in the college library. They asked him, "Today you look so sick. Have you caught a fever?"

He said, "For the last two or three days I have been feeling unwell and since last night I seem to have a fever as well."

When he came out of the library I was standing there. I said to him, "You look very sick."

He said, "Today I won't teach any classes. I have just come to inform the departmental head that I am not well and am going home." And he did not walk home. He called a horse-driven cart and went home that way.

In the evening all of us went to his residence. He was lying in bed running a high temperature. I asked his wife to check and it was a hundred and two. I said to him, "Now get up! This fever is not real."

He asked, "What do you mean?"

I said, "I have brought with me all those people who this morning had asked you whether you were feeling alright."

Seeing them he was astounded and he got up from the bed. He said, "What do you mean? I don't get it."

I said, "This way I am helping you to see Krishna. This temperature you are running is simply unreal. Get up; you are not unwell at all. On this first piece of paper it is written that you said you were feeling utterly fine. On the second piece of paper it is written that you said you had been feeling a bit unwell since last night. On the third it is written that you said you had been feeling unwell for two or three days and since last night you also had a fever.

"You gave all these replies this morning within a span of one and half to two hours. And here you are lying in bed with a temperature of a hundred and two. What the thermometer is showing is absolutely fake. It is purely your psychological imagination and projection."

Through imagination one can get a fever, even die. Whatever you want to see, you can see it. This is certainly not assimilation of a thought. It is simply a thought enveloping your mind in dense darkness. Any appearances arising out of it will be unreal. You don't have to assimilate a thought. On the contrary you have to say good-bye to all thoughts so that your own thinking can emerge. Not the assimilation of thought but the emergence of thinking. There is no greater deception, there is no bigger mistake or error, than insistently inflicting someone else's thought, concept or imagination on yourself.

Certainly you can see God. You can very easily see Krishna, or Christ hanging on the cross, or Rama holding a bow and arrow, or you can see any god that comes to your mind or your imagination. But this "seeing" is not seeing the truth. It is simply an extension of man's own imagination – and man's mind is very powerful.

The human mind has great power and it can perceive even the most imaginary thing. Women have more of this power than men, hence they can see God more quickly. Poets have more of this power than ordinary people, hence they can see God very quickly. The songs devotees have sung for God, the poetry they have written, are not coincidental. These are poets who have gone astray and became devotees, but they are basically poets. Their imagination is sharp and intense. They have gone astray, and now their poetry has turned toward God. Their imagination has turned toward God – they can see God, they can talk to God and they can walk holding his hand. For them, there is no problem in it. But all this is simply a pathological state of mind; it is not at all a healthy state of mind.

There are many ways to attain this sick state of mind, and if you want to attain it, there are a few ways to help you. Thousands of monks and sannyasins have been taking drugs like opium and hashish so that they could attain this sick state of mind, so that they could see God. All over the world sannyasins and devotees have got into numerous kinds of intoxications, into a dull and drunken state of mind, with the intention of encountering God more quickly. Don't be surprised by this. If you observe a fast for a long period, your mind becomes lax and sick. It results in the same chemical changes in the mind – slackness and feebleness – as drugs do: your imagination becomes sharp and it is easy to hallucinate.

You may have experienced that if you are running a high temperature and have not eaten for a few days, your mind starts imagining all sorts of things. It starts flying in the sky along with the bed, it starts touching the sky. Who knows what it starts seeing? Who knows what ghosts and devils come and stand around you?

The imagination of a sick mind, an unhealthy and weak mind, is sharper and more intense. The more pathological the mind, the sharper the imagination. There are many ways to make the mind sick. One way is by observing long fasts. Then the mind's efficiency starts fading, the body's capacity starts waning, and, in the absence of food, some vital elements essential for the body get exhausted. The body goes through a chemical change. That change is the same as the chemical change that takes place when drinking alcohol. It is the same chemical change that also takes place when you take drugs like mescaline and LSD.

If not today then tomorrow, we will be able to understand the whole chemistry of man's body, man's organic chemistry. It wouldn't be surprising if it were proved that fundamentally the same chemical changes happen in the body when observing a fast or through intoxication. As a result of those chemical changes, man's imagination becomes sharp, becomes very intense. In that intense and sharp imagination you can assimilate anything, you can see anything.

Perhaps you may not know that all the great poets, great novelists, and great dramatists are prone to fantasizing: they all go on seeing their characters.

We all are well acquainted with Tolstoy.

One day, Leo Tolstoy fell while climbing the stairs to a library. The staircase was narrow. At that time he was writing a novel called *Resurrection*. One of the female characters in the novel was climbing with him, although physically she was not there. Tolstoy was talking to her. A man was coming down the narrow staircase. There was enough room for two people to pass comfortably, but not for three. If all three had been men, they might have managed to pass. But it was difficult for two men and a woman. Thinking that the woman should not be squashed from either side, in a bid to save her, Tolstoy lost control, fell down the stairs and broke his leg.

The man who was coming down was amazed. He said, "Why did you try to squeeze past me? There was enough room for two of us."

He said, "What, two? There were three of us. One of the characters of my novel was with me, and trying to save her I fell."

This is not just the one incident. This has happened with all poets, all novelists, and it has been happening with all the imaginary people of their world.

The neighbors of Alexandre Dumas, the French dramatist, were often amazed.

Once he moved house in Paris. The people in the old area had become well acquainted with him, but not the people of the new one. On the very first night after his move he started a sword-fight with someone inside his room, in such a way that the people in the neighborhood were disturbed. There were two different kinds of noises coming from the room, but they doubted that there were two people inside. The swords were hitting against each other noisily. The neighbors informed the police that something strange was going on inside the new tenant's flat. On this dark night, his doors were locked and inside swords were hitting against each other with a loud noise. Also there were two very angry voices coming from the room.

The police arrived and they broke open the door. When they saw Alexandre Dumas standing alone with his sword, they were amazed and asked, "Where is the other man?"

Dumas came to his senses and asked, "Which other man? Oh, forgive me! That was just one of the characters in the play I am writing where a duel is taking place."

"But we could hear two voices coming from inside."

He said, "First I spoke on his behalf, then I spoke on my behalf!"

For Dumas the other person was very real. Had Dumas become a devotee by mistake, gone on the path of devotion, it would have been very easy for him to see God. Had Tolstoy become a devotee, just as the character from his play was walking beside him, similarly Lord Krishna or Rama or someone else could have walked beside him. There would have been no problem in it and no difference either.

Man's mind is imaginative. Constant repetition of any thought or concept creates self-hypnosis and what is imagined can manifest. But this is certainly not the experience of truth. Truth emerges; it cannot be assimilated. Tomorrow I will tell you how your mind can become empty of all thoughts and attain a state of no-thought. That alone is meditation and that alone is enlightenment. Any experience in that enlightenment is truth.

As long as you have just assimilated a thought it cannot be your own. Only when it arises from within, when it is born within you, can it be your own. And that will only happen when you say good-bye to all assimilated thoughts, to all concepts. Only someone who has become silent, empty of all concepts – who has become concept-less and free of thoughts – attains his own thinking, his own experience, his own truth.

So you are not to assimilate a thought; thinking has to emerge from within. It is the processes of assimilation which has kept God out of man's life and destroyed religion. Religion has simply been reduced to a game of imagination rather than a search for truth.

Just today someone came to me and asked:

Osho,
The devotees have seen God. If we don't chant the name of God, how will we see God? If we don't visualize a statue of God, how will we see God?

It is good not to have visions of God because there is no sense in getting caught up in delusions or imagination. Yes, it is possible that the dream may be very sweet, may look pleasant to you. But a dream is still a dream. Imagination is imagination, no matter how much happiness it may seem to bring. And anything imagined which makes you happy is more dangerous than something which makes you miserable. Why? Because it is easy to wake up from a fantasy which makes you miserable, but you don't want to wake up from the fantasy which gives you happiness; you feel like sleeping even more.

Blessed are those who have unpleasant dreams because they will feel like shattering those dreams. And unfortunate are those who have dreams which are utterly pleasant because they don't feel like waking up from those dreams. That is a simply fatal, poisonous, and intoxicating state.

So I am not telling you to assimilate any thought, concept or fantasy; rather I am saying that when you say good-bye to all concepts, all thoughts, all fantasies, what remains is your consciousness. When a question arises in that consciousness, when your consciousness is faced with a problem – the naked problem, the naked question – the answer, the solution, will simply arise out of your own being. Then there will be no effort to find an answer because the answer will not come out of your imagination and memory, but out of your very being. That solution will be your own experience; it will be your own thought. A thought does not become your own through assimilation. It cannot; there is no way that it can.

Someone has asked:

> Osho,
> You tell us to think, but what will happen just by thinking? When I go on thinking and thinking I simply get drowned in my thoughts. My conduct does not change, it remains the same. Tell me how to change my conduct.

Ordinarily it is said that the value of thinking – if there is any value in it at all – lies in a person's conduct. This is a lie and nonsense because deep down conduct is nothing but an expression of the thinking state. Where there is no seed of thinking, there cannot be a plant of good conduct. Yes, it is possible that fake behavior may be imposed from outside. But fake behavior has simply no value except that through it you can deceive other people, but your own life is destroyed.

You have asked, "…what will happen just by thinking?" Why have you asked this? Why has this question arisen in you? I can tell you: up until now, thinking has not been born in you. You take others' thoughts to be your own. Hence the problem of creating a harmony between thinking and conduct has arisen. If it is your own thought, it is impossible for your conduct to be contrary to it. If it is your own thought, then conduct simply follows the thought like a shadow. Just as when a bullock cart passes, the marks of the wheels appear, similarly wherever thinking emerges, lines and marks of conduct appear. You don't have to force good conduct, it comes of its own accord.

The thinking state is the center, the thinking state is the being and the thinking state is the soul, but we don't have any thoughts of our own. We have learned only thoughts that are borrowed. We have accumulated stale and leftover thoughts and we consider them to be our treasure. But good conduct does not arise out of those stale and leftover thoughts, hence the difficulty, hence this question arises: how to create a harmony between thinking and good conduct.

This is utterly foolish. Where the question of creating a harmony between thought and good conduct arises, you can know that this thought must be stale, old, leftover, another's, not your own. All these thoughts – you should speak the truth, you should love, you should love your enemy as yourself, you should not cheat or lie to anyone, you should not commit adultery, you should have no desires and lust – have been borrowed from others. Your conduct is totally contrary to them, so you have become disturbed and upset and ask how to create a harmony between thoughts and conduct. There just cannot be because there is no way harmony can be created.

It is fundamentally essential to know that your conduct is your own but your thoughts are from others. If you are a thief, that conduct is your own. The thought that non-stealing is religious and that it is a great virtue not to steal is simply another's thought. The conduct is yours but the thought is someone else's, so how can there be harmony? The thought could be from Mahavira or Buddha or Krishna or from Christ, but the conduct will be your own.

Mahavira's conduct was in tune with Mahavira's thinking; it followed it like a shadow. You may have borrowed a thought, but where will you borrow the conduct from? You certainly cannot borrow Mahavira's conduct or Buddha's or Christ's, but you can borrow their thoughts. You can have their thoughts for free, but not their good conduct. The thoughts are of these great people but the conduct is your own.

So there is a big gap between the two and this creates conflict, great pain and suffering. All around the clock a constant conflict is going on inside you; you are unnecessarily in hell. You may take a vow every day, you may observe a fast every day, you may go to the temple every day and make a resolution, but it won't make any difference; your conduct remains the same. If the thoughts are from others, how can these things make a difference?

When he finds himself in such a conflict, the first decision that a wise man will take is: "For the time being I will consider my conduct to be my real existence; this is what I am. Why should I accept someone else's thoughts? Why not search for myself? Why not think on my own? Why not use the experience of my own life? Why should I not silently dig within my own being and find out what is there?"

Have you ever dug within yourself? Have you ever looked into every single layer of your life? Have you ever tried to search within yourself to find out why anger cannot bring joy? No, you will just say that anger is a bad thing. But you are simply repeating someone else's words. The day your being experiences on its own that anger is poisonous, that anger brings misery and pain, the day your being is filled with the anguish of suffering and the poison of anger, will it then be possible for you to become angry?

When you have been angry, have you ever sat silently in a corner, closing all the doors, and tried to find out what anger is doing to you? In that moment, have you watched your being becoming scorched in the burning fire of anger? Have you seen what is happening inside you when you are burning with that anger? If you had even once looked inside, and even once seen the whole burning sensation and scorching of the anger, all the pain and hell would have become clear to you. Then who could persuade you to go into anger again?

But no, you have never looked at it. Once the anger has disappeared, the smoke of anger has evaporated, you sit reading the Gita, or the statements of Buddha or Mahavira, and you think: "Anger is a very bad thing. I am doing such a bad thing; I should not be doing it." Then you are in a dual difficulty – one of anger and another of repentance of anger. Both the anger and the repentance hurt us separately, but the repentance is meaningless because once the anger has gone, there is no way you can see the anger. If you had seen the anger when it was there, with all your wisdom and thoughtfulness, that seeing would have given birth to the experience of knowing what anger is. And that realization, that knowing, would have changed your whole conduct.

I am not telling you not to repent becoming angry, rather I am telling you to watch the anger. It is the idiots who repent. They can repent for their whole life but that won't help. Do you know why you repent? – it's not because anger is bad. You repent because when you become angry, the thought of how miserable and wretched you are comes as a shadow. Once the anger has disappeared, subsided, you realize that you have proved to be a bad person, you have abused someone badly, used such indecent words. Then your ego gets hurt because you think that you are a nice person who cannot say such indecent things.

It hurts your ego, so just to indulge and embellish your ego, you start repenting. You go to the temple and make a vow that you will never again become angry. By making such a vow you become a gentleman, a non-angry, nice person once more. But again you become angry and again you repent. This repentance is not about being angry, it is about restoring the image you have of yourself. How could I have stooped so low? It is the restoration of the part of the ego that has been hurt. Whenever the ego is shattered, it needs to be puffed up again.

All these vows and oaths – I will observe celibacy, I will never again become angry, I will do this or that – are substitutes for the ego; they serve no purpose. They are utterly fake and pseudo. Certainly, something *can* happen, not by repentance, but by being aware. Whatever situation grips your mind, be alert, wake up, and try to look at the situation, try to identify what is happening. And if you see pain and suffering, ignore it. Who wants pain and suffering? Only fools! But we have never really looked.

I can tell you with certainty: you have been angry many times but you have never watched your anger. You may say "I have been angry so many times, how could I *not* have watched it?" If you were capable of watching it, you couldn't be angry. The fact is: when you are angry, the ability to watch vanishes completely. In anger, you are in a state of complete drunkenness, in a stupor, unconscious. When they are in a state of anger, people can do things which they cannot even imagine doing when they are conscious and silent.

Thousands of murderers have maintained in the courts that they did not commit the murder. Earlier the courts used to think this was all lies. But now psychologists say they are telling the truth. They had killed in such a fury of anger that they were not at all conscious of what they were doing; they were almost unconscious. Afterward they couldn't remember that they had murdered someone. Psychologists say that they are not lying at all. Many murderers could not recall later that they had committed the crime. They were hanged, they were given life imprisonment – rotting away in stinking cells for their whole life – but they just could not remember that they had murdered someone. They kept saying that they just couldn't recall when they did it. Who would remember it? In the state of mind in which they murdered someone, there was barely any consciousness within them.

All sins are committed in a state of unconsciousness. When do we repent? We repent when the unconsciousness has disappeared, so there is no connection between the two. We commit the sin in a state of unconsciousness and when we are conscious we make a vow to be virtuous. There is simply no relation whatsoever. Hence every day we fall into a ditch – into the same ditch we decided yesterday we wouldn't fall into ever again. Every day we come across the same ditch, ten times a day. Then we lament, repent and think, "Mahavira, Buddha, Krishna, and Christ must have been real awakened ones. That is why they could go beyond anger. But how can we go beyond it? Every day we decide not to be angry and every day we fall back."

No, they were people just like you. None of them is a god, none of them is a *tirthankara*, and none of them is a son of God. They also had the same bones and flesh as you have, they also had everything that you have. They were born just as you are born and they died just as you will die. They had nothing special. In this world no one is special, all human beings are the same.

We find this more than surprising: how can a person attain such a state that anger disappears from his life? That no fire of lust burns inside him? That no hatred or jealousy arises in him? I say to you that it can happen in everyone's life. But we are unacquainted with how to achieve it. The whole science is not to condemn your conduct on the basis of other people's thought, but rather to observe your conduct, watch it, be alert and aware of it.

Don't call your conduct bad, because a man who calls it bad is unable to see it. If we call a person bad, we would not want him to come to our home, we don't even want to see him. So when you call an action bad, a wall is created between your mind and that action. Don't call anger bad. You have no right to call it bad, just as you have no right to call your stealing bad. Just try to find out what that stealing inside you is. Try to identify it in total silence, in total neutrality. Try to investigate: what is anger? What is sex? Why is it there? What is it? Watch it in silence, observe it with indifference and without any condemnation. The day you attain this seeing naturally, a revolution will happen in your life. That day your own thinking will be born. Then your conduct will not be contrary to that thinking; it can never be.

This is why I don't tell you to create a harmony between your thoughts and conduct. Please don't ever try to create this harmony. Your conduct is a reality. Whatever your conduct is, watch it, as out of that the true thought is born. And it is that true thought which creates the revolution in your conduct. Then without any projection, without any enforcement, without any suppression, you experience a new man awakening inside you. It is the reflection of the thoughts that have arisen out of your own experience.

There are a few more questions which I will discuss tomorrow. Now we will sit for the night meditation. Before we sit, let me tell you a few more things about meditation.

In my view, meditation is not doing, it is not an effort. Hence if you make it an effort, you won't be able to go into meditation. Meditation is just relaxation: no effort is needed, no striving, no trying, and no fighting inside. It is not like someone swimming in a river. If a person is swimming, he has to continuously move his hands; he has to fight the current, make an effort. But meditation is not like swimming.

Then what is meditation like? Meditation is like floating. It is like a person simply lying in the river and floating. He neither moves his hands, nor fights the current. He remains lying quietly and the current carries him along. He makes no effort whatsoever; he simply floats. Meditation is not like swimming, meditation is like floating.

Don't swim, float. For fifteen minutes drop all effort and striving. Don't try to find ways, don't try to *do* anything – I should sit this way, do this, think this or concentrate my mind this way – don't do any of this because if you do, you will never be able to go into meditation. Anything that comes out of your effort cannot be bigger than the mind. Anything that comes out of your effort will be a part of the mind. Meditation is not part of the mind. Neither inhale forcefully nor hold your breath nor make any effort.

So what should you do? Just sit very relaxed. It is not even necessary to sit. If you are experimenting, you can lie down, or you can even stand if you feel comfortable. You don't have to sit in any particular posture or like a statue; you can sit in any way. The real issue is your inner state of mind not your posture. Never, even by mistake, get into childish things – if I sit this way I will become God or an awakened one. If I point my nose this way or stand on my head, then this will happen and that will happen. Never get into these kinds of childish things.

Meditation does not have a deep connection with the body. Meditation has something to do with your inner state of mind. Hence let go of your body in a way which is the most comfortable for you so that the body does not create a disturbance. This is enough as far as the body is concerned.

What should you do within? You have neither to remember a name of God nor chant a mantra. You have neither to concentrate on a fixed point nor visualize the flame of a burning oil lamp or a flower blossoming in your heart. You don't have to get into these kinds of fantasies. You don't have to visualize any beautiful scenes, heaven, hell, or the underworld. You just have to sit in complete silence; you have to be awake and aware of all that is happening around you.

All this may be happening: a train may be rumbling past, an airplane may pass in the sky, some bird may flutter in the leaves of a tree and make a noise, someone may cough, a small child may cry, someone may walk about. All around you things will be happening. You have to be silent and aware of all these happenings lest any incident escapes your awareness, lest even the faintest sound escapes your awareness. Your awareness should be alert; you should be fully conscious. Whatever is happening around you, you should experience it, should feel the sensitivity of it, should know and identify that it has happened.

But you are not to start *thinking* about it. If a dog barks, you are not to think: whose dog is barking? Is it white, black or red? You are not to think of all this. If a dog is barking, its bark will just echo inside you, it should echo in your awareness, then fade away. Let it come as it comes, and when it disappears, let it disappear. Whatever comes inside, let it come and go. Inside, thoughts may go on moving. They will not necessarily suddenly calm down this very day.

For thousands and thousands of years, mankind has been nourishing and feeding thoughts. They are very old guests, they have been staying at your house for a long time. You have been feeding and nurturing them your whole life. So no one should be under the delusion that if they sit in meditation today, all thoughts will disappear. They can come, they will come. They don't know that you have decided not to call them anymore. You have been calling them all these years, so they simply come, thinking that you are calling them. They come out of old delusion, out of old love.

So there is nothing to get nervous about. Let them come. Go on watching them silently. Just as they came, they will go. How long can a thought stay? It will come and go. Just carry on being a witness. Here the thought will come, there it will go. You are neither to prevent it nor to discard it, saying: "Disappear! From where has this thought come and disturbed my meditation?"

Meditation is not something that can be disturbed. When meditation happens, nothing in the world has the power to disturb it. And if it does not happen, then you are already disturbed, you are already in mess; it is not your meditation that is getting disturbed. When meditation happens, it just cannot be disturbed. The question of disturbance does not arise.

Don't bother about your meditation getting disturbed by a thought coming. The thought has come, it will disappear. Why does it bother you? Just go on silently watching it. You will feel the breath going in, going out; just watch it. An insect may bite you and you may have to remove it with your hands. Let your hands remove it, then continue watching silently. You are not to force anything, you just have to be aware of one thing: whether you remove the insect, or move your feet, or open your eyes in the middle, or a thought comes, or a dog barks or a bird chirps, keep this in mind: "I am listening to everything, I am watching everything in awareness."

When we burn a lamp, the lamp radiates light on everything around it. Similarly, inside you the lamp of awareness should remain lit and all that is happening around should be illuminated, the light should fall on everything. Slowly, slowly within five to seven minutes, silence starts descending. If we can accomplish just this much awareness, an unprecedented silence will descend.

Just today a friend told me: "For years I have been constantly trying to find ways to be silent, but nothing happened. I did this and I did that, but nothing happened. Yesterday when I just sat down in awareness, I was amazed at what happened. It was beyond my imagination." It will happen and it is going to be something beyond your imagination. You just won't know it. Whatever happens will be totally unknown and unfamiliar, you just cannot expect it to happen. You won't even be able to figure out what will happen.

You cannot predict what will happen in meditation nor can you imagine it. Whatever happens will be unique. You have never known it. It is absolutely unknown, but it will only happen when your known mind becomes absolutely silent – and it *will* become silent.

So everyone has to sit very silently, very effortlessly, and without straining himself. Everyone has to sit silently and comfortably at a short distance from the next person. When someone is touching you, it is as if you are sitting in a crowd. Then it becomes difficult. Give all everyone a bit of space. Never mind if they have to sit on the grass, that's no problem.

Today we will switch off the light so that you can be totally alone in the darkness. Just wait for a while until the light is switched off. First let everyone be seated, then we'll switch it off.

Just keep this in mind: no one should be touching you. If someone is unnecessarily touching you, your attention will be diverted. I'll assume that all of you are sitting in such a way that you are not touching each other.

[*Someone comments that there is not much space available.*]

There is always more space. You need to have the courage to spread out. Okay, so you have understood my point.

Close your eyes and sit very comfortably. As it will be dark, it won't be a problem; no one will be watching you. Otherwise you may be afraid all the time that someone is watching you. People have strange kinds of fears, and the greatest fear is that someone is watching them: who knows what he might be thinking? So we will make it dark.

No one is watching you; you are completely alone. Watch yourself, don't bother about others. And don't try to find ways to look at another person. Keep your eyes closed. You have to close your eyes gently, don't close them tightly. That creates tension in the eyelids. You have to just let go of the eyelids gently as if your eyes have gone to sleep. You have to drop the eyelids gently. And then sit silently very relaxed and light, like a flower.

It is an amazing night. If the deep silence of the night can descend on you, then right now something will blossom inside you like a flower, like a lamp. You can experience something within. Don't miss the opportunity. Be absolutely silent, relax your body and sit without straining yourself in anyway.

Close your eyes. Close your eyes gently and let go of all the stress in your head. It is the head which is the most burdened. Relax the lines on your forehead. Let go of the burden on your head as if you have put the whole burden down. Keep your face absolutely strain-free. Just as small children have no strain on their faces, similarly make your face strain-free. Try to remember how your face was when you were a small child and let your face now be the same; let it be as relaxed and loose.

Wake up within, be completely awake within, fully conscious within. Sit so alert and so sensitively that you can hear even the faintest sound, the slightest sound, any sound. It's as if a lamp has become alight inside; you are fully conscious and awake within. Now try to listen, be fully conscious and try to listen. For ten minutes be utterly silent.

You are sitting absolutely alone, totally alone, as if you were sitting in a dense forest. The night is utterly silent, full of deep silence. You are sitting totally alert, you can hear even the faintest sound, the faintest noise. You are fully awake. Slowly, slowly the deep silence will start descending. Slowly, slowly your mind will become more silent and you will even start experiencing the breath. You will start feeling the vibrations of the breath. Watch, go on watching. Listen, go on listening. Your mind is becoming silent.

Watch, look within, everything is becoming silent. There is deep silence outside and deep silence is entering you. Every single layer within is becoming silent. Watch, watch in awareness within, slowly, slowly your mind is becoming silent. An unknown silence is descending.

Your mind is becoming silent. Slowly, slowly your mind will

become completely silent. Just be awake, everything is becoming silent. Slowly, slowly your mind is becoming silent; an unknown silence will start descending – it *is* descending.

Silence is descending. Each and every layer of your mind is becoming silent – a shower of silence. Your whole mind is bathed in this silence. Watch how the mind goes on becoming even more silent; understand this. That alone is the key.

The mind is silent. Slowly, slowly the mind will become totally silent. You will be erased; you will be completely erased. Only silence will remain.

CHAPTER 6

religiousness: understanding life

In the last two days we have contemplated on two states of the mind. On the first day I talked about the thought-less state. The thought-less state is born out of beliefs and faiths, and those who envelop themselves in the thought-less state are deprived of knowing truth. Yesterday we contemplated on how the thinking state can be born in us.

Only minds free of beliefs, faith, and blind trust can manifest at the thinking state. Only in those minds which show so much courage that they can destroy the traditions and the blind concepts given by society can the thinking state be born – a state which brings freedom and moves them toward truth. Today I will talk a little about the state of no-thought.

Before I talk about what I mean by no-thought, I must say a few things about how we are in trapped in a web of thoughts. Around the clock, man's mind, in some way or other, is surrounded by a fabric of thoughts. A crowd of thoughts keeps moving inside us; sometimes we are aware of it, but most of the time we aren't. It's as if some action is going on inside us, a race is going on inside us. If we become totally aware of that race, we may get frightened; we may think that some madman is sitting inside us. If even for an hour we remember the mesh of all the thoughts going on in our mind, then tremendous anxiety and anguish will arise in our life.

Very few people are aware that inside them there is a confusion of thoughts, a crowd of self-contradictory thoughts, a web of thoughts in conflict with each other. In this conflict and inner friction the whole energy of man's mind gets exhausted. And if someone's mind energy gets exhausted, he becomes so weak within that there is no possibility for him to move on a search for truth. Before he moves on the search for truth and the experience of life, he must get rid of this constant depletion of energy at the level of the mind. He must conserve this energy and be free of the conflicts of the mind.

You may never have thought about this, so once in a while just sit alone and write down whatever is going on in your mind – be honest, write it down, whatever it is. And in that one hour you will see that your mind is woven like a cobweb. You will find things there which you never even imagined or expected could be inside you.

There will be devotional songs. There will be nice words like *soul* and *God*, but there will also be abusive language. There will be the most hateful and abhorrent feelings, and the desire to commit the most heinous crimes. On seeing such desires you will be shocked. There will be no connection whatsoever between the thoughts. They will be totally unrelated and contradictory to each other. Your mind will jump from one thought to another, it will jump from one desire to another. If in that one hour you write down whatever is going on in your mind, exactly and with all sincerity, you will start thinking: Am I mad?

As far as I can see, there is no fundamental difference between a madman and an ordinary man – there cannot be. The madman is someone born inside us; it is simply our own growth. Considering the state we are in, any one of us can become mad any moment. The difference between us and the madman is not qualitative; it is only of quantity, of degree. If the heated and feverish thoughts running inside increase by just a few degrees, any one of us can go mad. There are very few people in human society who are sane. Most people are – some more, some less – in a state of madness. We aren't aware of the level of madness that is acceptable in the day-to-day functioning of life; we don't even think about it. It is only when that madness tears us completely away from our normal daily lives that we become aware of it.

In such a neurotic state of thoughts, how can one move toward truth? And I'm speaking to *you*, nobody else, I am not telling this to anyone else, I am only telling you this as it is utterly essential to know this fact: in a state of extreme tension and anxiety this web of conflicting and self-contradictory thoughts, self-contradictory feelings, makes a person insane.

You will not be surprised to know that most of the people considered to be great thinkers went mad. Hence when someone says that Mahavira was a great thinker or Buddha was a great thinker, I really feel like laughing. Neither of them were thinkers. They were people who had attained a state of no-thought. They were standing at the opposite pole from where you can go mad. Insanity is one extremity of the mind and liberation is the other – and all of us keep swaying somewhere between the two.

If the tension and burden of thoughts go on increasing, we move toward the point of insanity. If the tension and burden of thoughts wane, the mind becomes more calm and silent. If we can reach a state where there are no ripples or vibrations of thought whatsoever, then we are closer to being liberated. These are the two points of the human mind – liberation and insanity. Whatever we do in life, ordinarily we go on moving toward the point of insanity. Religiousness and meditation invite us to move in the other direction. So the first thing is to become aware of the fact that we are either mad or close to the point of going mad. Unless we wake up to this fact, the urge to get rid of this state cannot be born in us.

Dormant madness is moving inside us. If we get a shock, our madness will manifest on the outside. It is hiding inside us. Even our closest friend does not know what is going on inside us. The wife does not know what is going on in the husband's mind; the husband does not know what is going on in the wife's mind. It is present inside us like a disease. And we keep it hidden and suppressed, we don't let it manifest. But the moment we get a great shock – some loved one dies, our house catches fire, we are bankrupt, or we lose all our prestige – that which is hidden inside us like a wound simply bursts open and our madness manifests on the outside.

And it is not that only one person is suffering because of this madness from within, the whole society is suffering. This madness has collective expressions as well; this madness causes a collective upheaval. Sometimes this madness grips the crowd, it grips the whole society, the whole country, and the whole of mankind. Wherever in the world there are Hindu-Mohammedan riots going on, or a person from one community is fighting with someone from another community, or an Indian is fighting a Pakistani, or countries are fighting each other, these are feverish expressions of collective madness. When all the madness moving inside people becomes too intense and there are no individual ways to release it, it manifests collectively.

I would like to tell you this – you may have never thought of it – that when a war is going on in the world there is a drastic reduction in the number of people going mad. When it happened during the First World War, psychologists all over the world were utterly puzzled: why did this happen? During the First World War, the average number of people going mad fell, the suicide rate dropped, and there were less murders and other crimes than normal. During the Second World War it was even stranger. Suddenly the suicide rate dropped considerably, the number of people being murdered and going mad fell drastically. That time psychologists became very interested, and there were great discussions about why this was happening.

In a situation of war, people's madness gets released collectively, so the number of people going individually mad reduces drastically. And this is the reason why you also find so much energy all around when there is a war going on. Whenever there is a war, people become utterly delighted, their faces start radiating, and a kind of momentum, intensity, comes into their lives. They look very happy. During the time of war they wake up early in the morning, read the newspaper, listen to the radio, and then talk about the war with everyone they meet during the day. A kind of great excitement comes into their lives when a war happens. Why? – war is an outlet for the release of our individual madness.

If two people are fighting on the street, you leave all your important work and start watching the fight. Why? – because this is an opportunity for the release of your inner madness. Wherever there is violence and hatred, wherever there are riots, bloodshed or murders going on, or when thrillers are being screened in a cinema, you feel a lot of energy just by watching them. Why? The energy flows because when you see all that is going on inside happening outside, you feel a relaxation, the tension inside you lessens. That is why every five to ten years a great war becomes a necessity.

Even if a politician tries a million times, war cannot be avoided, peace cannot happen in the world; he is just banging his head against a brick wall. Unless steps are taken to reduce each individual's madness, wars will continue; only the reasons or the excuses will change. Earlier, people used to fight in the name of religion, now they fight in the name of nations, in the name of languages, in the name of -isms and ideologies, and in the name of communism and democracy. The issues will change, but the fighting will continue.

The history of the last five thousand years has shown us that wars cannot be avoided. No matter what the politician says, no matter how much he appeals for peace, no matter how much he shouts that there has to be peace in the world, peace cannot happen. It won't happen until we understand this fact: war is not a political matter, but rather the result of individual madness becoming so intense, the minds of the masses becoming so sick, that the madness manifests collectively and there is no other outlet than war.

During the Second World War, sixty million people were killed and that gave us some relief. For ten to fifteen years afterward there was quiet. But since then the madness has accumulated again. Now we won't settle for anything less than killing a hundred or a hundred and fifty million people. If the madness continues to grow at this pace, then by the end of the century perhaps only when we destroy the whole of humanity will our madness find some relief. This tense and feverish-like state moving inside our mind diminishes our life in every way, it is life's complete downfall. Then the excuses could be anything, what the excuse is doesn't matter.

So how to transform this state of man's mind? How can a person move from the excessive crowd of thoughts toward the state of no-thought and silence? Today I want to say a few things to you about this. But before that, I had to describe to you what the situation is.

And remember: I am talking to *you*, not to anyone else. It often happens that when I tell you something like this, you will start thinking, "What he says is absolutely right. This is the case with people." If you don't count yourself, it is not going to solve anything. But that is how we count. In your minds, you must be thinking that what I am saying is absolutely right, that this is the case with those sitting next to you. But that will not serve any purpose. This is *your* issue and it has nothing to do with the person sitting next to you. You will have to rationally think about yourself: "Am *I* mad inside?"

If you are mad, then in this state of madness even being a Hindu won't make any difference, reading the Gita or the Koran won't make any difference. If a mad person reads the Koran, the world will be in danger, his reading will lead to danger. If a mad person reads the Gita, that reading will lead to danger. If a mad person goes to the temple, the temple will become a cause of trouble. If a mad person goes to the mosque, the mosque will create fights. No peace, no love, no enlightenment, and no truth can be born through anything that a mad person does. Whatever he does will lead to trouble.

Therefore, before a mad person does anything, it would be much better, essential and important, if he tried to understand his madness. He should find out if there is any way he can become free of that madness. Only then will everything he does be meaningful. Otherwise all these actions will prove futile. He will try to serve people but create trouble. He will talk of love but soon be at another's throat. He will talk of love, say "I love you," but soon you will find he has no love for you, that you have no greater enemy. It makes no difference what he talks about. He will talk of peace, but after a while he will draw a sword and say, "Now nothing else can be done to defend peace except take up the sword."

Didn't we hear in India recently about the need to defend nonviolence with violence? If a person is mad, he will even draw a sword to defend nonviolence, saying that now violence is needed to defend it. Anything that a madman does will take him deeper into madness.

Therefore, the first thing is to become aware of your own madness. And what do I call madness? – a mind which is in conflict, a mind which is surrounded by a crowd of thoughts so that it is unable to perceive anything clearly or make a decision.

Such a mind is either on the verge of going mad or has already gone mad.

Once, William James went to visit a madhouse. When he came home, he could not sleep the whole night. He got up again and again.

His wife asked, "What is the matter? Why are you so upset?"

He said, "I am upset because today I went to visit the people in the madhouse. On seeing them a fear entered me: could what has happened to them happen to me at any moment? Sleep has disappeared. I am feeling terribly scared, my whole being is trembling."

His wife said, "You are worrying unnecessarily. Who told you that you can go mad?"

William James said, "No one told me, I'm just assuming it. Today what I saw in their eyes, what I saw in their behavior... The thunderbolt that has fallen on them can at any moment fall on me too. I am the same human being as they are. Before they went mad they were just like me. There is no fundamental difference between us. So what has happened to them can happen to me as well."

William James lived for thirty years after that visit. He has written that he remained restless for all those years. He wrote, "Every moment I was scared that madness could grab me at any time."

I recommend that you go to a madhouse sometime and look carefully at the mad people. You will see your own image there. It is only a question of proportion. You will find that they are only one step ahead of you. As long as our minds are in conflict, as long as our minds are full of contradictions, as long as the contradictory thoughts are moving inside us, we all are in that same state of trembling which any moment can turn into an explosion.

So what is the path? What should we do? What can be done

to free our minds of conflict and of the crowd of thoughts? I want to give you three keys to contemplate on.

First: there is a great fear in our minds about becoming empty. We have been taught not to be empty because an empty mind is the Devil's house. This is what we have been told: an empty mind becomes the Devil's workshop, but I say to you: an empty mind is the house of godliness and a full mind is the house of the Devil.

This fear has been put on us: never let the mind stay empty, never be idle. So a fear of emptiness pervades; that is why we are never ready to be empty inside. We want to fill ourselves, keep ourselves stuffed with one thing or another. No sooner do we wake up in the morning than we start reading the newspaper. If we are alone, then we go out and meet friends, we go to a club, turn on the radio and television or start reading the Gita, the Koran or some other book. No one wants to sit and be empty because we have this unnecessary fear, this phobia, about emptiness. But is it irrational? Perhaps there is some reason behind it. Let me talk about this.

No one wants to be empty. We all have a fear of being empty. Around the clock we want to keep ourselves occupied. When there is no other choice, we drink alcohol or we listen to the radio or go to sleep as we are not at all ready to be empty. Why? Where does this fear come from? There are some fundamental reasons behind it.

The first is that if we sit and become empty – and our mind remains empty – we are afraid that slowly, slowly we will become nobody, that we are just nothing. We all have this desire to be somebody, hence the fear of becoming nobody.

Out of this desire – "I want to become somebody" – we accumulate wealth, and the more wealth I have, the more I will be somebody. Then I won't remain an ordinary person, I will become a special person. That is why we accumulate wealth, accumulate fame, accumulate power so that we can become somebody. And that is why we accumulate thoughts as well.

This race to become somebody takes us into all kinds of accumulating – and the most subtle is the accumulation of thoughts. A person who has too many thoughts, is full of too many thoughts, we call a pundit and we respect him. If someone has memorized all the Upanishads and the Gita, we say he is a blessed one. If someone has memorized all the scriptures, we say he is worthy of worship. We respect the accumulation of thoughts; we consider it to be knowing. Therefore we also collect thoughts: the more we collect, the more knowledgeable we will be, the more we will be somebody. It is this race and ambition to become somebody which doesn't allow us to be empty, which doesn't allow us to stay empty. It creates the fear in us that if we don't accumulate we will be in difficulty.

Christ has said, "Blessed are those who are poor in spirit." He has said an amazing thing: "Blessed are those who are poor in spirit." He has said a strange thing, because we all want to be prosperous in spirit. So why did he say this? Why did this thought come to his mind? To be poor in spirit means a man who is empty, who has nothing inside him – neither thoughts nor knowledge. But then why is he blessed? He is blessed because the moment he is empty, the moment he is ready to be a nobody from within, the moment he accepts his inner nothingness, in that moment he will know that he really is nobody. He will realize, "Why should I be in the race to become somebody? And by being in that race, will I really be able to be somebody? Could I ever be somebody?"

The day he fully attains this experience, this understanding that he is nobody and he becomes willing to remain nobody, that very day and in that empty space he experiences godliness, truth, life, or whatever name we want to call it. That very day, in spite of being poor, he becomes rich in a truer sense. That very day he becomes empty and that very day he is filled.

When it rains, the huge mountains which are already full are deprived of water; the rain simply falls on the mountainside and flows down into the deeper valleys. The valleys and ditches are filled with water and become lakes. The ditches that were empty become full and the hills which were full remain empty. Godliness is also constantly showering, raining – every moment. Life is also raining every moment. And those who are empty within will be filled and those who are full within will remain empty.

But we are all in the race to fill ourselves, we go on stuffing ourselves – from inside as well as from outside. Outside we accumulate clothes, wealth, and a house; inside we go on accumulating thoughts, scriptures, words. Inside we accumulate these things and outside we accumulate those things.

If ever someone is aware of this madness: "By filling myself with these outer things I still remain empty"... If ever the thought occurs to him: "By stuffing myself with those outer things, I will remain deprived of that which would make my being ecstatic, of that which would have given it immortality," he renounces his home, wife, children, but still does not drop all those words and scriptures that are stuffed inside him.

You cannot fill yourself with the outer home, outer friends or loved ones, but you *can* fill yourself with inner prejudices and inner thoughts. Only someone who is willing to drop them is a sannyasin. Someone who is willing to drop all the inner words and thoughts, he alone is a true renunciate, he alone is a non-possessor.

So the first key is nonpossession of thoughts.

Don't accumulate thoughts, drop them, let go of them. Then there will be only "that" within: not a thought, but your soul, your being, your existence, your authentic being. The whole web of thoughts should disappear, should be wiped out. Only that which is pure isness, pure being should remain. And what is attained in that lone experience of pure isness, in that empty experience of pure isness, that alone is truth, that alone is the soul and that alone is godliness – or any other name you want to give it.

We have a feeling of possession toward the accumulated thoughts. Right now I am speaking to you. You can go away from here and start accumulating my thoughts. But my thoughts being accumulated inside will only harm you; they cannot benefit you in any way. Inside you the crowd will increase further. Some people were already sitting inside you and then I will also be sitting there. As it is, there are already too many people, there is no space and now one more person will be entering you, more thoughts will enter; this will create a disaster inside you.

Don't have this feeling of possession toward thoughts. You don't have to keep accumulating them and gathering a crowd inside. You don't have to memorize them, you don't have to remember them. Then what should you do?

You have to have a sense of nonpossession toward thoughts. A sense of nonpossession means you don't want to store them. Understanding is one thing, and accumulation is a totally different thing. Understanding what I am saying is one thing, accumulating it is another. Understanding what Mahavira, Buddha and Krishna have said is one thing, accumulating it is a totally different thing. Understanding is not accumulation; in understanding there is no accumulation of any sort. Where there is accumulation, there is no understanding. Only someone who is unable to understand wants to accumulate. For someone who is able to understand there is no question of accumulation.

We only want to remember those things which we are unable to understand. If we can understand something, we don't have to remember it. There is simply no question of remembering it. There is simply no question of keeping it in the memory.

So don't have the desire to accumulate, have the desire to understand life. With understanding you attain knowing, with accumulation you attain scholarship. Scholarship and knowing are complete enemies. A scholar can never become enlightened and there is no reason for an enlightened one to become a scholar; there is no point. So you have to keep this fundamentally in mind.

"I am not going to accumulate thoughts." What is the sense in accumulating? All accumulation will be borrowed, it will be from others. Understanding will be yours, it will be your own. Accumulation will always come from others, will be stale and borrowed. Understanding is fresh, alive and young. Understanding liberates, accumulation binds. Understanding liberates you, makes you free. Accumulation binds you, it ties you in chains.

It is difficult for those people who accumulate words to understand; they don't understand anything at all. They cannot understand because understanding longs for liberation, for freshness, not staleness, not for anything borrowed. Accumulation makes everything borrowed. Even when those people look at life, their words stand between them and their looking at it. The words become an obstruction with life standing on the other side.

Once it happened in China…

A big fair was going on and it was very crowded. Right next to the fairground there was a well. There was no protecting wall around the well, and as it was so crowded a man was pushed into the well. The moment he fell into it he shouted, "Help! Save me!" But as it was so noisy no one heard him.

Later a Buddhist monk passed by the well and he heard the man shouting. He peered into the well and saw that the man was drowning. The man pleaded with the monk to save him.

But the Buddhist monk said, "My friend, you are suffering for your past deeds, so you'd better suffer. One has to suffer for past deeds. What will happen if I try to save you? Can anyone save anyone? Don't you know that in the scriptures it is written that no one can save anyone? Matter cannot change, water cannot become oil. So what can I do? If I somehow try to save you, by doing that I will get into a bind. It is better for you to suffer for the sins that you must have committed in the past, so that you will be free of them in the future."

The scriptures were speaking through him. Life was standing in front of him, someone was drowning, but the scriptures came in between.

The monk went away telling the drowning man, "Keep your mind calm. By keeping calm everything happens. And the calamity that has come upon you is the fruit of your past deeds, so suffer. By going through the suffering, they will cease."

The monk went on his way. The man kept shouting.

Next a monk who was a follower of Confucius came by. The man was still shouting and the monk peered inside the well and said, "Confucius has said thousands of times that if the state is not governed properly it leads to great trouble. This well has no protecting wall due to the inefficiency of the state. I will right now go and start a movement that the state should change hands, that there should be a revolution. All wells should have a protecting wall around them otherwise people are in trouble."

Although the man in the well was dying, the monk went to the crowded marketplace and started shouting. He gathered people around him saying, "Friends, come and see this lapse on the part of the state. Once the state goes wrong, everything goes wrong. Confucius believes that if the state is in the right hands then everything can be taken care of. Friends, look at the blunders made by the state. There is no wall around the well! Just look, that man is drowning."

Someone was drowning, dying, but the idea of rescuing him just did not occur to him. There was no way this idea could have arisen in him because Confucius' scriptures came in between.

After him a Christian missionary came past and he saw that the man was drowning. He immediately remembered Christ's words: "To serve a man is to serve God." He immediately jumped in and rescued the man.

You may think that this missionary did a very good thing, but no, he did not save the man either. There were also scriptures standing between him and the deed; he also did not save the man. He had no concern for the man's life. He simply jumped in the well and rescued the man for no other reason than what is written in the scriptures: to serve a man is to serve God. So here too the scriptures are standing in between; here too there is no life.

This story was written by a Christian missionary. But he is not aware of the fact that, even in the third example, the issue is the same as in the first two. The monks simply did what was written in their scriptures, and the missionary did what was written in his scripture. But all three had scriptures standing between them and life.

Look at life in all its multidimensional forms, understand it – the action that arises out of that understanding of life liberates. Only an action which comes out of an understanding of life is religious. But from everywhere words and scriptures create a wall between us and life. A pundit is unable to understand. This is why all over the world pundits belonging to different religions go on fighting each other. If truth is one, then religion is also one. But there are so many pundits, so many scriptures, and many kinds of sects. A pundit keeps fighting because he cannot understand the other person. His own words become an obstruction. His words come and stand between him and the other person. Then understanding becomes impossible. This foolishness leads to fights, leads to religious rivalries, and conflicts among religions all over the world. And these conflicts are born because a pundit is simply incapable of understanding.

Where there is understanding, there cannot be conflict. Where there is understanding, there cannot be rivalry or fighting. There will be love, there cannot be hatred. Where there is love, there is understanding.

So remember, no matter how many words, scriptures or thoughts you may accumulate, your understanding will certainly not grow. You cannot accumulate understanding. Understanding sees, is aware of issues in their totality. Out of that awareness, knowing is born in you. That knowing is not accumulation, that knowing is not accumulated anywhere. That knowing transforms your whole being, it purifies your soul, and makes it new. It gives you a new life. It is not a burden; it does not weigh you down. No wall is created between life and you.

Try to understand the mistake, the error, of accumulating thoughts. Remember: the less there is a crowd of thoughts within you, the sooner knowing emerges. The less thoughts accumulate within you, the sooner the liberating wind of knowing blows, and understanding is born in you. Then your life can move toward attaining the state of no-thought, toward enlightenment.

Hence I say the first key is: nonpossession of thoughts.

If you are nonpossessive toward thoughts, the second sutra will be inevitable: the attachment to thoughts will drop. Right now we say "It is *my* thought!" Which thought is yours? But if there is an argument you will say "It is my thought. My religion. My scripture. My *tirthankara*. My God." From where does this "my" enter you? Which thought is your own? Is there a single thought which is your own?

Just dig a little, do an analysis, try to catch hold of every single thought and identify whether or not it is yours. And you will find it is not yours; it has come from somewhere. It has come floating on the wind and has settled inside you. Where is the "my"? How can any thought be yours? It must have come from somewhere else; it must have traveled from somewhere else and become resident inside you. All thoughts are guests, not a single thought is yours.

Saying "It is my thought," creates an attachment to the thought; we become identified with it. Then we try to defend it, we want to preserve it, we don't want to let go of it. Once anything becomes "mine," we start trying to safeguard it. Then it becomes my wealth, my treasure; it becomes a part of my being.

You must become aware of and understand this fact: none of the thoughts are "mine." The moment it becomes clear to you that not a single thought is yours, immediately your attachment to thoughts will drop, the idea that they belong to you will drop. Once the feeling of "my-ness" toward anything drops, the link to that thing is disconnected. It is attachment that is the connecting link between you and that thing. It is attachment alone which is the connection. Nothing else connects thoughts with our minds, glues them to our minds; attachment is the only link.

If you are a Jaina and someone abuses the Jaina religion, then your being starts quivering: he has abused *my* religion. If you are a Christian and someone says something bad about the Christian religion, you immediately get ready to fight with him because he has condemned *my* religion. And all because you say "my thought." The "my-ness" immediately gets hurt and alerts your ego. Then you are even ready to die for that thought; you are ready to sacrifice your life for that thought.

Many people have sacrificed their lives for their thoughts. Many people have died for the sake of ideology. And there are also people who console those who are dying, saying "Don't worry, if you are dying for Islam, for the sake of the Hindu religion, heaven will be yours." Man has been taught any amount of idiotic things about dying for the sake of something – die for the sake of communism, die for the sake of democracy, die for the sake of a thought, become a martyr then every year people will gather at your tomb to celebrate – but he has not been taught anything meaningful about living.

When someone becomes ready to die, just think how deep his attachment will be. He is ready to lose his life for the sake of a thought and that thought is totally alien to him. And he is ready to lose his soul, lose his life for *that*? But our idiocies are deep-rooted, so we honor him: he did a great thing by dying for Islam or for the Hindu religion or for the Jaina religion; his sacrifice was great. But what is the reality? The reality is that he became so deeply attached to a thought that he was not ready to let go of it, but ready to give his life for it. His life was his own whereas the thought was absolutely alien.

When attachment reaches this extent, fanaticism is born out of this madness. The religious fanatics in the world have filled the whole earth with so many killings and with foolishness beyond description. And the only connection is that we have developed a feeling of "my-ness" toward a thought. Once it becomes ours, we are even willing to die for it because it becomes part of our ego.

If you want to become free from a thought, then you will have to break the link which makes a thought "mine." And you don't have to make much effort to break it because that link is utterly fake. It does not exist; it is just an idea, an imagination. None of the thoughts are your own. Can you tell me any thought that is your own? Which thought? No, it will be from the Gita, it will be from the Koran or the Bible. It will be from Krishna, Mahavira, or from someone else. Not a single thought is your own. All thoughts are alien, borrowed.

Forming an attachment to those alien and borrowed thoughts is to lay a foundation for trouble in the mind. Try to understand this truth: none of the thoughts are "mine." Hence no thought is worthy of you forming an attachment to it. As your understanding deepens, your attachment will start withering away. When you start seeing that all thoughts are alien to you, you will know that fighting and quarreling for the sake of a thought is like fighting with a shadow; it's almost the same.

You must have heard this story…

In a village, two pundits were standing by the side of a river. They had simply wasted their whole life in scholarly pursuits, hence they had neither fields nor a cow nor a buffalo. But both of them used to think of buying a field. So they were contemplating on each buying a piece of land on the other side of the river.

The first pundit said, "It is right that we buy separate pieces of land, but keep one thing in mind: no animal of yours should ever enter my field."

The second pundit said, "My dear friend, you just cannot trust animals. They may enter your field. How can I follow the animals around all the time to see where they are going?"

The first man said, "This is an impossible situation. It will simply ruin our friendship. I will not tolerate your animals entering my field."

The second man said, "So what will you do?"

The first one said, "I will kill the animals there and then."

The second man said, "Okay, where is your field?"

The first man drew a square on the ground with a stick and said, "This is my field."

Then the second man drew a circle next to it and said, "This is my field." He drew two lines with the sticks and said, "Here are my buffaloes." He had put his buffaloes in the first man's field. "My buffaloes have entered your field. Do whatever you want to do."

The first man made a cross through those lines indicating that he had killed the buffaloes.

The "buffaloes" were just lines drawn on the ground, but they got into a fight. The matter went to court where they filed a case against each other. The second man said, "He forced his buffaloes into my field and it is because of those buffaloes that we got into a fight, into beating each other."

The magistrate asked, "Where are the fields located? And where are the buffaloes?"

They both said, "Forget it. We have yet to buy the fields and there are no buffaloes."

A fight for the sake of a thought is almost the same as a fight about fields which exist nowhere, a fight about buffaloes which exist nowhere. It is only a fight about shadows, but shadows become so important that we are ready to give our life for them.

There must certainly be a very deep idiocy in man's life otherwise this would not have been possible. All those martyrs who died in the name of thoughts and religions must have been utter idiots otherwise it would not have been possible. This whole fight for the sake of thoughts is simply foolishness. That fight arises out of attachment. Because of attachment, thoughts stick to us and we go on accumulating them. All thoughts are given to us by others, but when it comes to dropping them our being starts quivering.

Bertrand Russell has written that sometimes, in moments of great wisdom, he feels that there has never been a greater man than Buddha in the world. But then immediately his being starts feeling afraid and he asks himself how Buddha can be greater than Christ. It is not possible. In those moments of great understanding, he has written that he feels that Buddha is a unique man, there has not been a greater person than him. But immediately something in him starts getting frightened because his childhood conditioning was that Christ is the son of God and there is no greater man than him. And he starts thinking: "No, no, how it is possible that anyone could be greater than Christ?" He has written: "I contemplate a lot on this, I understand everything, but still I cannot get rid of this thought."

Thoughts take hold of us in such a way that they become more important than understanding. I am not saying that Christ is lower or Buddha is higher. That is just foolish; no one is higher or lower. But thoughts take such a strong hold on us, our attachment to them is so intense, that they override our understanding. Then we are willing to drop the understanding but not willing to drop the thought. This is simply a sign of madness. One should always be prepared to drop thoughts for the sake of understanding but one should never be ready to drop understanding for the sake of thoughts. Even for the sake of trivial thoughts we always drop understanding.

When India and Pakistan were divided, who were the people

who killed the Hindus, killed the Mohammedans? They were people like us, just the same as we are, people who visited a mosque or a temple every day, read the Gita and the Koran every day. But they just had these thoughts: "I am a Hindu" and "You are a Mohammedan." These two thoughts, these petty thoughts, that simply have no value other than that teaching, other than that, right from childhood, it has been bred into one person's mind "You are a Hindu" and into another person's mind "You are a Moham-medan." And they have both learned these stupidities; for the sake of them they forgot all their mosques and temples, the Koran and the Gita, and started poking knives into each other's chests.

They were people just like us! Even we could do it right now, we could do it right here: you could simply poke a knife into the person sitting next to you. And all your understanding would go down the drain, all your understanding would simply disappear. Just this one thought – the Hindu religion is in danger, or Islam is in danger – comes to your mind, and all your understanding disappears.

Thoughts have become more important than understanding because we have become too attached to them. We must com-pletely break this attachment – it is not difficult to break because it is absolutely imaginary. There is no such chain anywhere; it is only in our imagination. It is necessary to drop the attachment to thoughts.

So the first thing is: nonpossession of thoughts.

The second thing: dropping the attachment to thoughts.

And the third thing: be in a state of indifferent witnessing of thoughts.

The most important key is the third one. The first two are its background. The first two are its primary preparations. The third key is: a state of indifferent witnessing of thoughts. The extent to which someone attains a state of indifferent witnessing of thoughts, to that same extent, he attains a state of no-thought. If he can totally accomplish a state of witnessing, then no thoughts will come, all his thoughts will disappear – he attains enlightenment. What is meant by a state of indifferent witnessing?

Have you ever stood by the side of a river? Have you ever stood on the banks and watched? While you are standing or sitting there, the river continues flowing and you are just watching it. Have you ever sat on the ground and watched a flock of birds flying in formation in the sky? You are sitting there and the flock of birds is flying, but the birds don't belong to you, they are neither your friend nor your enemy, you don't admire them nor do you hate them – you are just watching them. You are watching the birds flying above you with a feeling of indifference. With that same indifference, you need to watch the thoughts that are lined up in a queue and moving inside you. Sit down – and just watch.

The thoughts are moving. No thought is yours, none of them is your enemy or your friend, none of them is a good thought or a bad thought. The flock of thoughts is flying and you are just sitting silently watching it from afar. You have nothing to do with it. It's the same as when people are walking along a crowded street and you are standing at the side watching. Watch the thoughts with indifference, like a witness, like someone standing far away from them, with no judgment as to whether they are good thoughts or bad thoughts, whether the thoughts are yours or another's.

Constant practice of it, constant remembrance of it, and constantly being in a state of such indifference will, step-by-step, lead to the diminishing of thoughts. Thoughts will go on flowing, but as you become more indifferent and the more you stand aside, amazingly the gaps between the thoughts will become longer, fewer thoughts will come, and the crowd will diminish.

They came because we called them. They were not incidental; they came by invitation. They were our guests, we invited them, arranged their stay and considered them to be our own – that is why they are there. The day we stop considering them to be our own, the day we become indifferent to them, neglect them, the day we become unconcerned, there remains no reason for them to stay. They start gradually slipping away, disappearing.

If you constantly try to achieve this – standing aside from thoughts with a feeling of indifference – one day, unexpectedly, you will find that thoughts have disappeared; you are alone. In that moment there is isness, but no trace of thoughts. There is a flame of isness, but no smoke of thoughts. The day pure isness manifests, there is not a single cloud of thoughts. In that state of no-thought you come to know that which is. In that moment you become acquainted with that which we may call godliness, truth, the root source of life, or any other name.

Only in that moment do you become acquainted with that which is your being. Only in that moment do you come to know that which never dies, which is immortal. Before that, nothing can be known. No-thought is the door to truth. A state of no-thought is the door to godliness. And in order to reach the state of no-thought, it is necessary to be a witness in every way. But it is difficult to remain a witness; we immediately become identified.

You must have heard of Vidyasagar, a great scholar and thinker of Bengal. He was an intelligent man, very well-read and he had written many books and many commentaries. In Bengal, there has never since been a greater scholar, a greater pundit, than he was.

Once he went to see a drama and in one scene the villain was chasing, and badly harassing, a woman. Vidyasagar was a gentleman through and through and he couldn't tolerate it. A moment came when that character finally managed to catch hold of the woman. Vidyasagar simply got up and threw his shoe at the man. He was sitting in a front seat and the shoe hit the villain. He said, "Stop, you scoundrel!" It was just a drama, but he simply forgot it.

The actor who was playing the villain must have been far more intelligent than Vidyasagar. He picked up the shoe and respectfully touching his forehead with it said, "I have never received a greater reward than this. I take it as a compliment on my acting skills that even a man like Vidyasagar started thinking a drama was reality."

We forget that a drama is a drama, and yet it is essential for us to know that life is also a drama. To us, a drama starts appearing to be life and yet we must recognize that life is a drama. Only then can we be indifferent; only when thoughts remain a drama moving on the screen can we stand a distance away from them. But right now our situation is such that even a drama immediately becomes a part of our life, we start taking it to be reality. While watching a movie we start crying and laughing, we start wiping our tears. And when the images moving on the screen envelop our being, it becomes utterly difficult to remain indifferent to them. But by constant and continuous wakefulness, by awareness, by right remembrance – and through meditation – indifference is not impossible.

So slowly, slowly learn to be indifferent to the minor things in life. Sometime when you are walking along the street, suddenly stop, and for a while just watch indifferently what is going on. Sometime when you are sitting with your family, for a moment just be indifferent but aware, and watch: everything that is happening is a drama. Whenever and wherever you are, for a while stop suddenly and watch: all that is happening is a drama. This way, slowly, slowly the ability to be a witness will grow inside you and you will then be able to be a witness at the level of the mind. The day you become a witness at that level, that day, that very day, a new world, a new door, will open in front of you. For the first time, you will become acquainted with life. Up until this point, we have been acquainted only with death.

On the first day I told you about death, that we are almost corpses, we are simply dying every day and we have no idea of life. Life is behind a locked door, encaged and imprisoned inside us. Unless we break that lock, it is difficult to go in and know life. That lock is thoughts, that lock is the identification with thoughts. That lock is attachment to thoughts, that lock is possessiveness about thoughts. If thoughts vanish completely, if this rush and web of thoughts comes to a halt, if your mind becomes silent, without any ripples, then in that wave-less mind we can know life.

Immortality dwells in every single person. And the energy of the original life source, the primal life source, is hidden inside everyone, though very few are able to become acquainted with it. But if someone makes an effort and longs for it, if he works hard and is resolved, he can become acquainted with it.

If you want to ask anything about this, I will talk to you this evening.

If you try to understand what I have told you about these three things – the thought-less state, the thinking state, and the state of no-thought – it will surely bring results.

I am very grateful to you that you listened to my talks with such love and silence.

about Osho

Osho's unique contribution to the understanding of who we are defies categorization. Mystic and scientist, a rebellious spirit whose sole interest is to alert humanity to the urgent need to discover a new way of living. To continue as before is to invite threats to our very survival on this unique and beautiful planet.

His essential point is that only by changing ourselves, one individual at a time, can the outcome of all our "selves" – our societies, our cultures, our beliefs, our world – also change. The doorway to that change is meditation.

Osho the scientist has experimented and scrutinized all the approaches of the past and examined their effects on the modern human being and responded to their shortcomings by creating a new starting point for the hyperactive 21st Century mind: OSHO Active Meditations.

Once the agitation of a modern lifetime has started to settle, "activity" can melt into "passivity," a key starting point of real meditation. To support this next step, Osho has transformed the ancient "art of listening" into a subtle contemporary methodology: the OSHO Talks. Here words become music, the listener discovers who is listening, and the awareness moves from what is being heard to the individual doing the listening. Magically, as silence arises, what needs to be heard is understood directly, free from the distraction of a mind that can only interrupt and interfere with this delicate process.

These thousands of talks cover everything from the individual quest for meaning to the most urgent social and political issues facing society today. Osho's books are not written but are transcribed from audio and video recordings of these extemporaneous talks to international audiences. As he puts it, "So remember: whatever I am saying is not just for you...I am talking also for the future generations."

Osho has been described by *The Sunday Times* in London as one of the "1000 Makers of the 20th Century" and by American author Tom Robbins as "the most dangerous man since Jesus Christ." *Sunday Mid-Day* (India) has selected Osho as one of ten people – along with Gandhi, Nehru and Buddha – who have changed the destiny of India.

About his own work Osho has said that he is helping to create the conditions for the birth of a new kind of human being. He often characterizes this new human being as "Zorba the Buddha" – capable both of enjoying the earthy pleasures of a Zorba the Greek and the silent serenity of a Gautama the Buddha.

Running like a thread through all aspects of Osho's talks and meditations is a vision that encompasses both the timeless wisdom of all ages past and the highest potential of today's (and tomorrow's) science and technology.

Osho is known for his revolutionary contribution to the science of inner transformation, with an approach to meditation that acknowledges the accelerated pace of contemporary life. His unique OSHO Active Meditations™ are designed to first release the accumulated stresses of body and mind, so that it is then easier to take an experience of stillness and thought-free relaxation into daily life.

Two autobiographical works by the author are available:
Autobiography of a Spiritually Incorrect Mystic,
St Martins Press, New York (book and eBook)
Glimpses of a Golden Childhood,
OSHO Media International, Pune, India (book and eBook)

OSHO international meditation resort

Each year the Meditation Resort welcomes thousands of people from more than 100 countries. The unique campus provides an opportunity for a direct personal experience of a new way of living – with more awareness, relaxation, celebration and creativity. A great variety of around-the-clock and around-the-year program options are available. Doing nothing and just relaxing is one of them!

All of the programs are based on Osho's vision of "Zorba the Buddha" – a qualitatively new kind of human being who is able *both* to participate creatively in everyday life *and* to relax into silence and meditation.

Location
Located 100 miles southeast of Mumbai in the thriving modern city of Pune, India, the OSHO International Meditation Resort is a holiday destination with a difference. The Meditation Resort is spread over 28 acres of spectacular gardens in a beautiful tree lined residential area.

OSHO Meditations
A full daily schedule of meditations for every type of person includes both traditional and revolutionary methods, and particularly the OSHO Active Meditations™. The daily meditation program takes place in what must be the world's largest meditation hall, the OSHO Auditorium.

OSHO Multiversity

Individual sessions, courses and workshops cover everything from creative arts to holistic health, personal transformation, relationship and life transition, transforming meditation into a lifestyle for life and work, esoteric sciences, and the "Zen" approach to sports and recreation. The secret of the OSHO Multiversity's success lies in the fact that all its programs are combined with meditation, supporting the understanding that as human beings we are far more than the sum of our parts.

OSHO Basho Spa

The luxurious Basho Spa provides for leisurely open-air swimming surrounded by trees and tropical green. The uniquely styled, spacious Jacuzzi, the saunas, gym, tennis courts...all these are enhanced by their stunningly beautiful setting.

Cuisine

A variety of different eating areas serve delicious Western, Asian and Indian vegetarian food – most of it organically grown especially for the Meditation Resort. Breads and cakes are baked in the resort's own bakery.

Night life

There are many evening events to choose from – dancing being at the top of the list! Other activities include full-moon meditations beneath the stars, variety shows, music performances and meditations for daily life.

Facilities

You can buy all of your basic necessities and toiletries in the Galleria. The Multimedia Gallery sells a large range of OSHO media products. There is also a bank, a travel agency and a Cyber Café on-campus. For those who enjoy shopping, Pune provides all the options, ranging from traditional and ethnic Indian products to all of the global brand-name stores.

Accommodation

You can choose to stay in the elegant rooms of the OSHO Guesthouse, or for longer stays on campus you can select one of the OSHO Living-In programs. Additionally there is a plentiful variety of nearby hotels and serviced apartments.

www.osho.com/meditationresort
www.osho.com/guesthouse
www.osho.com/livingin

The Tantra Experience: Evolution through Love
Tantric Transformation: When Love Meets Meditation

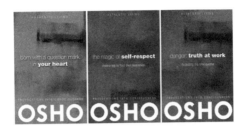

<u>**Pillars of Consciousness**</u> (illustrated)
BUDDHA: His Life and Teachings and Impact on Humanity
ZEN: Its History and Teachings and Impact on Humanity
TANTRA: The Way of Acceptance
TAO: The State and the Art

<u>**Authentic Living**</u>

Danger: Truth at Work: The Courage to Accept the Unknowable
The Magic of Self-Respect: Awakening to Your Own Awareness
Born With a Question Mark in Your Heart

<u>**OSHO eBooks and "OSHO-Singles"**</u>
Emotions: Freedom from Anger, Jealousy and Fear
Meditation: The First and Last Freedom
What Is Meditation?
The Book of Secrets: 112 Meditations to Discover the Mystery Within

20 Difficult Things to Accomplish in This World
Compassion, Love and Sex
Hypnosis in the Service of Meditation
Why Is Communication So Difficult, Particularly between Lovers?
Bringing Up Children

Why Should I Grieve Now?: facing a loss and letting it go
Love and Hate: just two sides of the same coin

Next Time You Feel Angry...
Next Time You Feel Lonely...
Next Time You Feel Suicidal...

OSHO Media BLOG
http://oshomedia.blog.osho.com

for more information

www.**OSHO**.com

a comprehensive multi-language website including a magazine, OSHO Books, OSHO Talks in audio and video formats, the OSHO Library text archive in English and Hindi and extensive information about OSHO Meditations. You will also find the program schedule of the OSHO Multiversity and information about the OSHO International Meditation Resort.

http://OSHO.com/AllAboutOSHO
http://OSHO.com/Resort
http://OSHO.com/Shop
http://www.youtube.com/OSHO
http://www.Twitter.com/OSHO
http://www.facebook.com/pages/OSHO.International

To contact OSHO International Foundation:
www.osho.com/oshointernational,
oshointernational@oshointernational.com